MW01609284

# Your Soul's Invisible Codes

## Unveiling Your Sacred Love Story

Dr. Marj Britt

**BALBOA**
PRESS

A DIVISION OF HAY HOUSE

Scripture quotations are from the Holy Bible, King James Version (Authorized Version). First published in 1611. Quoted from the KJV Classic Reference Bible, Copyright © 1983 by The Zondervan Corporation.

Balboa Press books may be ordered through booksellers or by contacting:

Balboa Press
A Division of Hay House
1663 Liberty Drive
Bloomington, IN 47403
www.balboapress.com
1 (877) 407-4847

Print information available on the last page.

ISBN: 978-1-5043-7499-6 (sc)
ISBN: 978-1-5043-7501-6 (hc)
ISBN: 978-1-5043-7500-9 (e)

Library of Congress Control Number: 2017902621

Balboa Press rev. date: 05/03/2017

# Praise for the work of Dr. Marj Britt

*"Marj Britt is one of the great mystical visionaries of our time and this groundbreaking work is one of the most important spiritual guidebooks I have ever read. A brilliantly crafted, poetic roadmap for unveiling the unique "Love Story" embedded in every Soul, this magnificent book is full of loving wisdom, kind guidance, and deep insight. I HIGHLY and ENTHUSIASTICALLY recommend it!"*

**Ramananda John E. Welshons, author of**
**One Soul, One Love, One Heart and *Awakening From Grief***

*"I first met Dr. Marj Britt towards the end of 2013 when she and Adyashanti engaged in a very spirited and esoteric conversation about awakening and the descent of Grace, via one of Adya's live video broadcasts at Cafe Dharma. I was intrigued by Marj. She was so delightful and enthusiastic - an extraordinary, yet ordinary middle-aged American woman. She seemed to be literally overflowing with joy. At this time I was feeling lost and broken-hearted about something that was very dear to me which had come to an end. I am a curious person and I like to explore new possibilities.*

*"I was one of a small team that brought Werner Erhard's work to Australia and I also founded The Hunger Project in Australia. So, when Marj invited us, during that satsang with Adya, to connect with her at Called By Love, I did. Marj's teachings and courses have been healing and incredibly interesting! I have loved taking the 'deep dives' with her as we explore new territory and the mystery of life as it unfolds.*

*"Engaging with Marj's teachings is a delightful and at times challenging adventure. I am learning new ways of looking at the nature of reality (consciousness, life, love) and how it's played out in my life and 'my' life in it. I have new practical tools to work and play with, e.g. identifying my natural and earned gifts of genius. Marj has much experience in developing curriculum and her work is grounded in real-life experience. I am inspired by her intellect, her joy and her enthusiasm. Marj is love fully expressed which calls for that from me."*

**Kerry Silcock**
**Canberra, Australia**

*"Marj Britt, and her teachings, have nourished, inspired, and helped to connect me to my own call by Love. Marj truly sees, knows, and lives as Love, and can't help but transmit that to her students. When I'm with Marj in person, or on a call, the plane of possibilities opens and my true nature responds with a gleeful yes! I always come out more expanded and better able to live my life more fully.*

*"Marj is a woman of wisdom, passion, open-heartedness, and delight, all wrapped up into one inspirational being. Every class I take, and each encounter I have, whether it be directly or indirectly, leaves me shaking my head in wonder at how she expertly transmits into me exactly what I need in that moment. If you're like me and want to learn to speak the language of love fluently, and increase your capacity to be that Love, I strongly recommend the Codes of Co-Creation."*

**Toni Monsey, PhD**
**Charlotte, Vermont**

*"From the beginning, whenever I listen or talk with Marj, it's like I am in touch with my future self, guiding me, very lovingly, gently, yet firmly. One day on the call, it was like everyone coming live to speak was like a*

*different aspect of me talking and all of them providing glimpses. All of them. If it was about healing abilities, being a vessel for love, looking for a purpose in a job or daring to enter an intimate relationship, even what Marj said about her dream, 'You have received the seeds of the Universe in the Womb of the Divine Mother. You are bringing forth, giving birth to the manifestation', it felt it was indelibly connected to my own emergence that now seems to move into rapid acceleration.*

*"I have participated in all the pilot tele-courses over the course of last year and I am still in awe of the unfolding miracles. The exercises and writing assignments became the nucleus of manifestation, and looking back I can clearly see inspiration turning into imagination and subsequently taking shape and form in my own life. Marj Britt & Friends have become trusted teachers and genuine guides on this exploration into the Unknowing. The Sacred Love Story of my Life is ready for another chapter!"*

**Michaela Trnka, MD**
**Vienna, Austria**

*"Marj leads by example, especially regarding showing the way of a life lived as a sacred love story. Marj's compelling nature has led me to explore my own life in ways that I would have never found, building on the past and preparing for a future that transcends and includes! A recent example of that is her suggestion that I take the STAGES Inventory developed by Terri O'Fallon. That experience and the session with Terri that followed, along with further discussion of the results with Marj at Terri's suggestion, have been extremely helpful to me in ways that are becoming 'way showers' into the future.*

*"I have heard the burning bush story many times in my life; however, on one morning call, I heard the words as words to me; and, I have removed my shoes, trembling on what might come next."*

**Charles Smith**
**Austin, Texas**

*"I met Marj back in the 90's and seeing her on Sunday mornings giving her talks is what kept me alive. I was new to the area and hadn't yet made any friends. I walked into Unity of Tustin and felt like I had come home. The whole church became my family. Marj was my friend and loved me unconditionally. I had to sit up straight and stretch my brain to grasp her sermons fully. She is so brilliant and yet easy to 'get'. I feel honored to know her.*

*"I talked to her the day before I was having a six-hour surgery and she asked me to 'see' a light shining down on my body and to just know that it was healing me. That made all the difference. When the surgeon was finished he came out and spoke to my husband in the waiting room… 'Your wife is fine, the operation was more successful than I even imagined. She has great bone density and I was able to do a better job than ever. Thank God.' Marj did that for me. Her love put me at peace. I thank her for always being a great teacher, minister and my friend."*

**Judith Driscoll-Ruth**
**Wimberley, Texas**

*"Dr. Marj Britt is quite simply a joy to experience. She is a divinely-inspired and passionately-creative expression of what it means to be called by love. Over the past year, she has been a core source of teaching (me) by example to maintain focus and compassion within many of my own creative concepts and expressions, in applications to my being and my doing, and especially in expanding my desire and ability to listen with greater joy to others, and particularly to the Silence from whence God and the angels speak unto us all. In short, she's one of my favorite muses, and a treasure beyond all measure."*

**Jay Steinberg**
**Author, Screenwriter, Composer, Concert Pianist**
**Phoenix, Arizona**

*"My spiritual awakening began in 1955 when I decided to be a missionary. While in college, I discovered I could be a missionary in every situation in which I found myself. I cut my teeth on things like Joel Goldsmith, Unity teachings, Association for Research and Enlightenment groups, and more. When I met Marj, I knew I was in the presence of such a special guide...a guide that only comes to a few.*

*"My awakening grew by leaps and bounds under her care. Without fail, every time I've entered into a new 'experience' with Marj, it is a scary place because I know my life will never be the same! I never know where we're going, I just know it is going to be a wild ride! It does take courage to climb into the rocket ship, but the sweetness of change is so awesome as we give ourselves to the experience."*

**Sey Jones,**
**Ponca City, Oklahoma**

*"Rev. Dr. Marj Britt is a gifted speaker and visionary, as well as a great lover of the Divine. She has been a highly experienced guide and mentor for many spiritual aspirants at Unity of Tustin and in Called By Love.*

*"She has frequently risen to the heights of mystical awareness while incorporating the deep significance of all of life's turmoils and trials. She has done this breath-taking accomplishment both for herself, using the decades of her own life-experiences, as well as for others, explaining the maps and methods she discovered to understand all the intricacies of our sacred journey from a soul level."*

**Arlene Mazak, PhD**
**Greater Los Angeles area, California**

*"I have been called by love. I know I am called. I also know I don't know why and what that actually means. How could I know this so definitively? Actually, who cares because the question itself came to me*

*through Marj. But it was my question to answer and the question now demands my attention. It is not demanding in a hard way but in such a way I know it is a sacred path question for me.*

*"I am a person who loves and I am called to know Love now on a deeper level. Wow. It is astounding to me. I may think I know exactly when, how and 'the what' of Love and at the exact same time I have known exactly nothing! I don't think I am alone. I am scared—I could love more but I hear that little tiny voice asking me to wait a moment. Don't go, stay with me safe here, don't love anymore right now, please stay here.*

*"BUT here I am called by love. So here I go. Others will be with me. I will go.*

*Dear Marj, that is who I can turn to. She Mystic, She Teacher, She Reverend, She Humorous with a wink, wink. No seriously, what can I say about someone whom I can bring such questions to. Imagine being able to trust someone on that level. Where you can start to question, ponder and play with the question of LOVE. Wow.*

*"Marj Britt thank you for being out there. I am no longer living in California but I hear you over the internet and take your classes. I am so grateful. Your student of a Life worth Loving."*

**Kathy Hill**
**Centerville, Maryland**

*"Dr. Marj Britt has led and guided me on an amazing spiritual journey for the last three years. Using my own life as a platform for gaining awareness of my soul journey has been an eye opening, embodied, divinely connected experience."*

**Caroline Bush**
**Norco, California**

*"Dr. Marj Britt, founder of Called By Love Institute, has been a Gift and an Inspiration in my life and a guide on my Spiritual Journey. Her gift of genius as a Spiritual Teacher is her ability to weave all the Sacred Traditions together and draw parallels between the major world traditions of East and West. In taking these sacred mystical teachings of Love and bringing awareness, we see the patterns and parallels interwoven in the stories of our own lives. We have the ability to see the points of Light and synchronicities as they occur in all the states and stages of our personal development and levels of consciousness. We begin to See through the eyes of God and hear the whispers of the Universe."*

**Vanessa Van Nieuwenhuysen**
**Tustin, California**

*"Dr. Marj Britt is a remarkable Master Spiritual Teacher, who serves as my role model for living a life from Love. She has the unique ability to translate the highest Mystical teachings into 'ordinary' language, so that you can integrate these into your daily life. Called By Love Institute is the culmination of her life's experience, ministry and Spiritual Work. Marj is dedicated to the evolution of consciousness of humanity and the planet. And Called By Love Institute is committed to helping those who are called to realize their gifts of genius and full potential. I am blessed to be part of this amazing team. Love is the ultimate reality!"*

**Nicolaas-John Van Nieuwenhuysen, MD**
**Tustin, California**

*"I am very blessed, humbled and grateful to be part of this great organization. Dr. Marj Britt has been an inspirational Soul in my life. Her teachings became and still are important instruments in my life. I discovered so much about myself throughout her teachings, guidance, and mostly how she shares from her heart, and the immense love she has for teaching, sharing her gifts*

*with whoever is open and willing, to journey with her. Dr. Marj is an amazing Master Teacher, a Luminary Mystic and a Mother."*

**Elizabeth Bruce-Lyle**
**Irvine, California**

*"Have you had experiences that touched you so deeply that you knew it went well beyond words, yet, your heart still had the desire to find a way to express it, somehow? The impact of Marj's presence, Love, support and teachings in my life is so rich that I can't possibly put it all in writing. And yet, through experiences and invitations, including those from this book 'Your Soul's Invisible Codes – Unveiling Your Sacred Love Story', I am finding more of my 'heart ways'. They are part of the alchemy happening inside of me.*

*"In 2013, a few months after meeting Marj for the first time, I asked her if she would be my 'American Mom'. She immediately said yes. Neither of us knew then that, shortly after, my life would change drastically. At a time when I didn't know what would be next, a series of synchronicities lead to what we now refer to as our 'Divine Appointment'.*

*"For the last three years, I have had the immense blessing of working with Marj, benefiting from her transformative guidance and support, while providing assistance for Called By Love Institute and Living, Loving, Legacy. This precious time has been filled with new points of reference and experiences. I am beginning to know what living Love without an opposite means, to understand and even find appreciation for my many 'holy tears', to continue going higher and deeper. It has involved taking leaps to express more of my Sacred Gifts, exploring in new ways the maps of consciousness and STAGES, while feeling progressively safer to know and be myself and to express it more. Numerous field trips are taking place, within and in the world.*

*"Being inspired by Marj leading the way in her own life, and her invitations through her book and Called By Love, I am loving the unfolding and am starting to express these Invisible Codes, which are becoming progressively more visible in my own life, in my own ways. It is inspiring some of my friends now to do the same. It truly is about harnessing the power of Love in our lives, in our personal expressions, with each other and in the world. There will be checkpoints and benchmarks, and the answer will always be Love."*

**Fabienne Meuleman**
**Executive Director of Called By Love Institute**
**Tustin, California (via Belgium, New York and more)**

# Dedication

To THE BELOVED souls who have been part of the mystery and the magic, the exquisite co-creation of the Campus of Consciousness that is Called By Love and Unity of Tustin, with the gardens this book highlights as the garden amidst the flames.

I have walked with so many of you through this garden. I have loved you deeply and felt your love. Many of your names are in this book, part of the stories. And this dedication is also to the unwritten names—they're also in the invisible—and to the parts of the love story that are still unfinished. My heart is filled with deep love and gratitude.

Beloved, I love you.

*O Marvel! a garden amidst the flames.*
*My heart has become capable of every form;*
*it is a pasture for gazelles and a convent for Christian monks,*
*and a temple for idols and the pilgrim's Ka'ba,*
*and the tables of the Torah and the book of the Quran.*
*I follow the religion of Love: whatever way Love's camel takes,*
*that is my religion and my faith.*

*—Ibn 'Arabi, "O Marvel"*

# Contents

## Timelessness Coming into Time:
## The Visible Dimensions
## Action and Manifestation

## Code 4: Will and Understanding:
## The Executive Power of Mind

## Code 5: Discernment and Choice

# A Monumental Leap: Multiple
## Realities Existing Simultaneously

## Code 6: Love and Wisdom: Mystical Union

## Code 7: The Realization and the Return

# Foreword by Andrew Harvey

FOR MORE THAN a decade, Marj Britt and I have shared a revolutionary vision. I have returned many times to the Campus of Consciousness that she co-created with her mystical community when she was the senior minister at Unity of Tustin, California for 19 years. We shared many deep conversations and entered into revolutionary and mystical teachings in the many multi-day intensives.

We walked the mystical garden path many times together. On one of those days I was telling her, "You must write", the poetry of 'A Garden Amidst the Flames' simply dropped into my awareness. I knew it would be part of the book that she would write. Now you can hold the book in your hands.

Marj has taken an evolutionary and revolutionary leap in the way that she has approached her writing. Each chapter is part memoir, part teaching and part practice. She uses the framework of the ancient Biblical story of creation, but not as she learned it in her childhood.

It blasts through the literal into the symbolic and lands in the mystical. It becomes a framework of the Stages of Co-Creation, with seven pillars, that weave in science and today's spiritual models such as integral, the spiral and stages of adult development. It takes us into the monumental leap and beyond.

The unusual thing is that Marj makes a radical commitment to this book being in ordinary language for ordinary and extraordinary people. It is authentic, self-revealing, filled with mystery and what she calls all of the colors of the rainbow. It is honoring of our entire journey, through all of the stages of our lives, with the awareness that everything works together for good when we are called by passion and purpose. She knows it as a childhood imprint of Romans 8:28.

Even as Marj honors the ordinary, she also integrates deep thinking and discipline. She has had the courage to go outside of the box, even though she is trained in the rigor of research skills, learned in the process of academic training, including a doctoral degree and dissertation from the University of Massachusetts.

In this simple, yet deep work, Marj uses her own deep-dives, earned as she collaborated with other great designers of maps and researchers of consciousness, relating to evolutionary and revolutionary change. I have been honored to be one of her co-creators, not only in live intensives, yet also including her first telesummit, www. LivingLovingLegacy.com, where she was in dialogue with some of the world's leading spiritual teachers. There will be more to come.

Sometimes, somehow, a higher and universal force manages to catapult people into greater levels of visionary vastness. That happened for Marj in reading some of my words in *The Way of Passion, a Celebration of Rumi*. I wrote: "Set up educational institutions in which the sacred role of genius can be really known and understood and in which mystical discipline becomes the foundation of all the other disciplines." It became a personal mission statement for Marj and her vision.

This mandate ignited a clear awareness of passion and purpose as Marj continued in her years of leadership at Unity of Tustin, as well as serving on the worldwide Unity Seminary board for many years. That passion now ignites www.CalledByLoveInstitute.com, as her focus shifts from a bricks and mortar platform to the invisible platform of a worldwide Campus of Consciousness.

What Marj has written is a revolutionary and evolutionary book of a different kind. There are things that are pivotal in her vision. First there is a total honoring of scholarly research that interweaves silently with her commitment to writing in ordinary language. She deeply integrates all of what she practices and teaches as stage developmental theory, calling it dancing all of the colors.

With a mystic's heart and voice, Marj invites people to spiral higher and deeper, shine their light in the darkness and step out with radical trust and faith, becoming part of a greater vision for our own lives and the world. It is about embodied love, in our relationships, our work, our passion and our purpose.

There is an audacity in the way she writes, letting you in on some of the secrets that mystics have known for thousands of years and giving you practices to access them. She talks of downloads coming in the stillness or the silence or other ways as natural. She guides you in seeing the way that synchronicity and intersections in time work, bringing us into co-creative relationships. You will be invited to pay attention to your dreams with the awareness that they can bring divine assignments, directing you and affirming you, even when we question, wonder or even feel discouraged or disappointed.

The teachings are brilliant as they integrate creative and unusual constructions in Marj's field of passion. She sees unusual connections between different fields and invites you to see them also. Then she guides and invites us in how we can develop and co-create constructions that will be of benefit to self, those we love, our communities and our world.

This book is about shifts in ways of perceiving and seeing, shifts that will open into the creation of new, rare and elegant models of co-creation. Marj knows that some may find her commitment to ordinary language and love as a conveyor belt as naïve and too simple. Yet, in her passion, she sees a magic that holds the promise of solving many of the struggles from which humanity is suffering.

For Marj, love and Awareness of awareness is what will bridge the gap. What you will find, if you can enter with non-attachment to your own language and say yes to the practices, is an invitation to bring your own gifts of genius into the process.

Andrew Harvey, Oak Park, Illinois

# Introduction

IT IS ALMOST impossible to put into words what this body of work means to me. It is equally difficult to express the love that I feel for the souls to whom it is dedicated.

Life has given me many gifts of passion and purpose. My last great passion is storytelling. For me, it is the way to unveil your soul's invisible codes, and in the process also find your own sacred love story.

My scribing started after I experienced my beloved passing through the veils. I had known him since my teens. As I felt the shock and the loss, I needed a way to find my own life again, a way to move through the grief. He was not only my beloved; he was my deepest soul connection.

That is when the scribing began. It became a way to experience what I was feeling, a celebration of the love even as I felt numb with the loss. I had been a spiritual teacher, a facilitator of the evolution of consciousness. Now I was being given another gift of "how," for myself in my deepest need. It is now being offered to you, perhaps in a time of need or yearning.

It is about symbols and images, all of the colors of the rainbow. They came in dreams, in memories that dropped in, in awareness of teachings that became very personal, not just of the cognitive mind. The elements are in the stories, in the illustrations, and the titles. They are all related to the living energy of love and the memories I have of times together.

I wanted to write words that people would project onto their own lives, feel as visual flavors and colors of their own experiences. It would be a way to bridge the gap between the visible and the invisible, a glimpse of forever love. It would be my own way back, through the grief that can envelop us when loss occurs in our lives.

There were moments when I pushed myself to transparency, not always feeling safe. I would come back to remembering that nothing can be more safe or lasting than cosmic love.

There are more pieces of the mystery. It has included going outside of the box, sometimes breaking rules or expectations. Let me share a relevant example, simple and perhaps strange.

For many years, in my writing and spiritual teaching, I have been a rule breaker when it comes to rules for capitalization. I have capitalized words when writing, and even spoken of them as with a capital, illustrating a knowing of a higher vibration. This included words like spirit, realization, higher self, or higher power, words of mystery. It worked for me as I wrote and taught.

We can even find this differentiation in the Bible. God is always capitalized. Occasionally, however, we will find it is not. Jesus asks a question, found in John 10:34, "Is it not written … you are gods?"

I transcended rules as a shorthand way to indicate a higher state or stage of consciousness. Now I find myself embracing and including another reality, one with capitalization rules that are part of the landscape I am entering, which includes the *Chicago Manual of Style*. There is an inner pause, as I take a deep breath, knowing that a shift is occurring within my own being. I will write and I will trust you to know or intuit the significance of the terms, particularly in the context of how they're used. We will be explorers, mapmakers and guides together.

One of the significant imprints in my life comes from short verses from the Bible that I learned as a child. The Bible that I still use is the King James Version. There are many translations; it's like different languages for different countries.

You may not have had that influence and may have imprints that work for you, maybe movies or even children's books. Use whatever works for you, especially if it comes in one of those downloads or dreams that I talk about in the glimpses of this journey that we are embarking on together.

One of the greatest reasons for me to self-publish this book, which I very consciously chose, is that I needed some control of how the words might be edited. I know it will be a field that is rare, often not understood. So much came in the form of downloads. That made my choice simple; the words had to remain pure, as they were given.

I needed the book to reflect all of the colors of the rainbow that would be reflected in the details that I would write. My awareness at different stages of my life has been different. I needed to find people in publishing who would honor what I now know as Awareness of awareness.

There are forty usually short chapters, written with the thought that you might read and work with one chapter a day, or maybe one chapter a week, really letting it imprint, scribing and writing as you feel it. Giving yourself days of rest, part of the creation story, it could take a year. The number forty is a sacred number, a symbol, found in scripture. It took the children of Israel forty years to enter the Promised Land.

Jesus spent forty days in the wilderness, before beginning his public ministry that included the shift into resurrection. Ernest Wilson, a significant Unity writer, called it *The Week That Changed the World* and wrote a book by that title. It was Easter Week, on Palm Sunday, in 1993 that I first spoke at Unity of Tustin, titling my talk after the book by Ernest Wilson.

## A Campus of Consciousness and the gardens were to be born

I'll never forget the Friday that I drove onto the campus at Unity of Tustin for the first time. There were no cars in the parking lot, which ended about where the sanctuary begins now. All of the back area was orange grove. The sanctuary itself was small; the building would seat only eighty people, built by a congregation of about forty people.

It was April, in the springtime. I had been invited to become a temporary minister of a ministry that was in crisis. When I got out of the car, before the president of the board arrived to meet me, I was greeted with the smell of orange blossoms, which was coming from where the gardens are today. Suddenly I felt a sense of the sacred that enveloped everything. And I remembered my mom telling me that when she and my father got married, she wore orange blossoms in her hair. I was feeling a deep soul connection.

I saw the old Victorian house and realized that it was the one that I had seen in a deep time of visioning and meditation when I was in ministerial school at Unity Village. There were about fifty students in my class, which included some of the people who would become amazing leaders in ministry. Our teacher, Janet Manning, was guiding us in asking for a vision of where we were being called in ministry. Many of my classmates got visions of big churches, lots of people. All that I got was an old Victorian house and an awareness of the ocean. I had looked for that old Victorian house all over Northern California when I was the minister of Unity of Walnut Creek. Now, nearly a quarter of a century later, I have written a book about these gardens that I have loved so much.

This meditation garden and these sacred grounds mean so much to me. It is like they are part of my being. It's not that I'm attached; it doesn't feel that way. It sort of feels like they are another container for a part of my soul! I would imagine that some feel that way about their hometowns, perhaps, or other places and settings that have had very high meaning.

## Symbols, cosmic vibration, dreams, parables and templates

The garden is filled with symbols and images that all hold the profound power of cosmic vibration, as well as all of the colors of the levels of vibration as we ascend in awareness in our soul journey. I love to call it the colors of the rainbow. At the site in between Sites 1 and 2, it is depicted with chakra symbols, all identified in our human body by Charles Fillmore, cofounder of Unity, as he showed where the power centers are located. He called them the twelve powers.

The twelve powers are all part of the garden, what I call in the book the Codes of Co-Creation. The days of creation, or stages and states of involution and evolution, are foundational teachings of Unity. The book title, *Your Soul's Invisible Codes*, subtitled "Unveiling Your Sacred Love Story," is an invitation into the mystery and the power of this garden, what I refer to as a garden amidst the flames. That phrase is from a twelfth-century Sufi mystic; the story is in the book.

I receive a lot of guidance, or inspiration, from dreams. That was also one of the powerful ways that Charles Fillmore received direction and vision. The name Unity actually came to him in a dream. There are so many stories I've heard, mostly passed by oral tradition by people who knew him, that are about dreams. I've become deeply committed to the practice of paying attention to what emerges in dreams!

Jesus taught in parables. The parables are stories that can be understood on many different levels. It is all explained in scripture. One example of an explanation is found in Matthew 13:10–17: "To some has been given the gift of knowing the mysteries, to others, the gift is not yet given." It is the purpose of parables to know and give the mystery.

I believe that our lives are sacred love stories, if we are able to see our stories through the eyes of love. That is not always easy. Sometimes we see; sometimes we don't. My attempt is to write in ordinary language for ordinary and extraordinary people. It has to be simple. This will not be a scholarly book. There are already lots of those, of which I have read, studied, and even taught many. This needs to be a book that ordinary people could pick up and read, the people who don't ever read those scholarly books.

You are extraordinary, or you would not be reading this! The template we will use to understand the mystery is a creation story, sacred writing thousands of years old. It guides me. There is some kind of mystical power in the "thousands of years" part. You may find your own templates that will guide you. I've found others that interweave with mine, like integral, the spiral, the enneagram, and the research on stages of development.

## The Mystery of Love

This is about the mystery of love. And there are invitations for you to be part of it, to bring your life into the curriculum. It is centered, in part and in my heart, around the garden, which is also the garden of our lives. It involves stories, not ego stories but parables of the soul.

The stories are fragments of a love story. Each piece, or short chapter, is part memoir, part teaching, and part practice. The practice is the invitation for you to apply it and see it in your own life. It is a journey without distance. The practice ultimately could be the most important part. It's the part you write; it's your love story. It is an invitation to bring your own life into the curriculum. It is an invitation to write your own manifesto of love.

I believe in a very simple way that love can change our lives and ultimately the world. Love has a quality to it that is very rare, like the Pearl of Great Price. In its pure essence, it is like light that dissolves darkness. Many of the people who could potentially read this will think that I am naïve and that it is ridiculous to believe the simplicity of love could change the world. The seeing that I am inviting you into is a rare gift. I am aware that this may be writing for a future time.

Yet, in the scribing of what comes, for me and for you, if you say yes to the practice, we will be seeing through the eyes of love, seeing though the eyes of our souls. There will be a sowing of seeds in this seeing that holds the potential of a higher love birthing in us, in others that are part of our lives, and even in the world. I believe this kind of practice can heal. It has been said that this kind of healing can encompass seven generations into the past and seven generations into the future. There is mystery in this field that we experience as love.

In the simple stories is the complexity of the vastness. Each fragment is a hologram, a container of the All That Is, for those who have the eyes to see. The walk through the garden that we will share unfolds in three phases or tiers, even though all of it is invisibly contained in each stage. They are called "days" in the creation story. You will become skilled at seeing both the visible and the invisible. The three phases or tiers are actually part of our lives and part of the evolution of our world. They have been called by many names. They include: the invisible and the timeless; the journey of manifestation; the realization and the return.

They show up differently, depending on where we are in our own process of perception. There are no wrong answers; there are only ways of learning, growing, and awakening. Ultimately, we see multiple realities existing simultaneously. And maybe you already do now. Even beyond that, all of it dissolves back into simplicity, and that is getting way ahead of ourselves for now! We'll start at the beginning of the garden ...

It has been a treasure to work with Karina Rindt, a gifted artist and photographer. She brought her own gift of genius, her passion and her art to the albums of pictures that she took for Called By Love. Now her gifts of photography and graphic design are part of this book. Karina had been part of my Mystical Bible class for many years. She was deeply involved in the beginnings of Called By Love. She knows me, and she knows my heart as well as my work.

It is about trust. I know that Karina understands all of the dimensions of the journey. I can trust her gifts of genius to reflect my own. We can be in dialogue about the why of dark, light, and color. A synergy of co-creation became the we-space gift of working together in the textures of our individual and shared passions.

## An invitation to Revelations of your heart's deep yearning

The words are imperfect, I am sure. Yet I wanted to bring together what some will see as fantasy, the glimpses of a reality that are vaster than the usual realities that we call our lives.

I wanted the whole process, what it was like to be there, experience the dazzling colors of all the stages of our lives, the joy and the sorrow, what I was feeling as I lived in the world of doing and what's happening now.

For me, it is so much more than a memoir or a teaching. It is an invitation to practice, a sacred practice, in the art of awareness.

I want this to be a book that people read and love, because it is their own story. My hope is that you will hold it and handle it in the ways of your heart. Highlight and write in it as you scribe your own stories, either in the book or a separate journal.

If pages get turned down, I will celebrate, knowing it is because it is important and you want to be able to find it again. If you draw stars in margins, as I do, it may be because something lit up and you felt it, inwardly knowing, *Oh my God, that is what is happening to me.*

There will be direct links back to times you experienced with people you have loved, to souls who loved and still love you. You will remember them loving you as you experience the feelings and the colors of the moments in time.

Your experience of what you may scribe will be a gift from your heart to the souls you love so much. If you write, it may be a legacy that you give to generations to come. And I also know that when you give, it will be given unto you. You will be giving a gift of love. It will return to you.

The essence of beauty will be the ultimate gift. There will be stories and pictures that people will share with each other. I can't think of a more perfect way for peace to come to the world.

The practices at the end of each chapter will have the invitation for writing, or what I call scribing that comes from beyond the rational mind. It sort of feels like it just drops in and comes from your heart. This is an important part if you choose to take the deep dives that reveal your soul's journey. There will be questions. Not all of them are meant to be answered; they are there only to be options, pointers that could guide you into deeper meaning.

It will be about you choosing one, or weaving together perhaps two or three. Or something completely different may come that is entirely your own. Most importantly, it is connecting with your heart, feeling your choices and beginning to see priorities that may be your own most important. Your heart will tell you.

Here is the first example. See if anything lights up and seems to call you. Listen for what comes; write words without judging. Just let it reveal what may be there.

Most of all, this is a love story. It is not about writing a masterpiece. You will receive glimpses, perhaps of your heart's deep yearning. If you connect with it, know that it will guide you, always.

## Practice: Bringing Your Life into the Curriculum

Take a few moments to center in the stillness of your very own being, knowing the beauty and the essence of your soul. Breathe deeply several times—slowly in, pausing, slowly out. Feel the energy of the All That Is in your heart.

Open now into the awareness of your life as a sacred love story, knowing that it will come and reveal itself to you.

What fragments came to you? Perhaps fragments that were beautiful or not, perhaps some you did not understand, perhaps some that changed.

What do you believe about love? What do you believe can change your life and even the world?

What have been some of the templates that have guided you in your life?

How have these templates come in and interwoven? How might they interweave with your sacred love story?

How do they become synergistic, part of something that is future time coming in, so you can in some way be a guide to a greater whole?

# Where We Begin

## The Invisible and Timeless Dimensions

*"This is a course in miracles. It is a required course.*
*Only the time you take it is voluntary.*
*Free will does not mean that you can establish the curriculum.*
*It means only that you can elect what you want to take*
*at a given time.*
*The course does not aim at teaching the meaning of love,*
*for that is beyond what can be taught. It does aim, however,*
*at removing the blocks to the awareness of love's presence,*
*which is your natural inheritance."*

*A Course in Miracles, Introduction*

# CHAPTER 1

## *Manifesto of Love*

WHERE DO I begin ... to tell the story of a love that never ends? To give words to our double spiral of life ... where every ending is a new beginning? How does it weave together, all of it, the joy and the sorrow, the love and the loss, the peace and the unknowing that is beyond our understanding?

How do the perfect souls simply show up in our lives in the ways that our own learning and growing, our dissolving and becoming, can unfold in our pathless path with both choice and destiny?

I've come to trust, radically trust, the many colors, the many dimensions of love in this love story without end. Timelessness has given me time, it seems, in which to decipher and see facets of light and darkness, at least in my own life, that are beyond my understanding.

What I know is that there are codes in the mystery. And they are codes that, if we are willing to see higher and deeper into our lives, we can begin to understand and know their ways. We will all begin to find our own ways of entering the vastness of our unique and individual mysteries that are part of the one.

It's like there are many paths that lead to the mountaintop. And when we reach the top, if we are above the clouds, we can look into the vastness and see that there are many mountaintops.

We will also find moments in time when we recognize that we are, or were, on or off the path. Points of new beginnings emerge, sometimes out of what has seemed to be darkness. Such a moment occurred in my life … now more than thirty years ago. It came as a surprise; I didn't plan it. For me, it was when what I've come to call the "Codes of Co-Creation" penetrated my very being.

I knew that my life had changed. It was like a flash of lightning in the night. There was a living flame of love that was beyond understanding. It took me into the journey without distance. My body tingled even as my mind dissolved.

I somehow knew there was a territory and there was mystery. There were veiled clues related to this territory that has seldom been seen and only rarely mapped by human minds. Somehow I knew my life's work would be about this. And the awareness of the details was not there, only a knowing that was as a glimpse.

Each of us has our own gifts of such moments in time. Sometimes we recognize them; other times we don't. Sometimes we say yes to the invitation; other times we ignore it, discount it, or even run.

Yet these glimpses are numinous, coming from dimensions beyond our human understanding. If we are willing, we may perhaps come to know them as our soul's calling, our destiny, calling us to a greater, higher, and deeper plan.

You are invited to an odyssey, one in which you participate, where you bring your own life, your soul's yearnings, into the journey. In some ways, it will be a memoir seen through the eyes of the soul. In other ways, it may involve glimpses of a future that exists, always already. If you say yes, you will participate at whatever level your heart tells you. It will be up to you …

There is a map that has imprinted itself in my heart and mind. It has become, for me, an invisible guide. It is an ancient map, based in ancient scripture in part. It has been and is sacred in the hearts and minds of millions of people around the world.

There are other parts of maps that have become deeply imprinted in my being. Some of them may weave their way into our unfolding tapestry. You will find your own maps from your own imprints weaving themselves in your experience.

Some of the weavings and wanderings on this unusual quest will be part of what I call Codes of Co-Creation. My deepest desire is that we not get caught in our human minds and that we follow where our hearts lead.

I've found significant pointers in this mystery. They have revealed themselves over my lifetime in different stages and ways. If you are willing to say yes to the exploration, it will happen for you also.

In that ancient scripture, they have been called the seven days of creation. The simple understandings have taken on deeper meaning as revelations have come in this play between the visible and the invisible. Stages or even mystical awareness now seem a vaster way to describe and glimpse their essence.

The number seven has vast meaning in itself as part of the mystery. There are seven days in a week, seven-year cycles and seven colors in the rainbow. There are seven chakras, or seven notes in a musical scale. Seven is mentioned 735 times in the Bible, it is a number of completion. It will be a magical and powerful guide to us as we begin our exploration of mystery and vastness beyond.

Let's begin with how it works, how we will explore these stages that represent treasure beyond measure.

1. **Let there be light**: recognizing the faces of love in your life

2. **Knowing in the unknowing**: knowing faith and radical trust in your own gifts of genius

3. **Glimpses of the soul**: downloads from beyond the rational mind, from creative imagination and Source

4. **Timelessness coming into time**: will and understanding that is greater than us, yet we are uniquely a part of it; knowing the bridge between human love and cosmic soul love

5. **Choice or no choice**: sea changes, upheavals, angels and sea monsters

6. **Mystical marriage and the union of heaven and earth**: love and wisdom; seeing with vertical awareness; multiple realities existing simultaneously

7. **Realization and return**: love without an opposite, joy and a peace that passes understanding; embodying your true voice—I Am That I am; returning to the marketplace with gift-bestowing hands: your soul's plan leads and guides

It will be in simple language for ordinary and extraordinary people. I don't know where the path will lead us. I do know some of the places it has taken me in my own life. They will be part of what I align with as we begin …

# CHAPTER 2

## *Moments in Time*

How DOES ONE describe a moment in time that descends into your life? It seemed simple and even ordinary at first, and then it wasn't ... Do I talk about sitting in a classroom that I had not expected to be in? Do I write about feeling lost in the world? Do I move to following the dots to find an unknown way?

The ship of my second marriage seemed to be crashing on the rocks. It was a marriage that I did not want to end. I had an imprint from my childhood that marriage was supposed to last. I had already been through the end of my first marriage even though it was my own choice. Or was it?

Sitting in the prayer chapel at Unity Village, Missouri, I was waiting for an appointment with someone who had called me to talk about the problem. My second husband was a minister, and dissolving marriages can be difficult for the churches they serve. I felt embarrassed, even some shame, yet most of all, just plain lost.

I clenched my hands into fists, struggling with the feelings, wanting to pray to somehow fix it all. A memory verse from my fundamentalist childhood of learning about Bible stories, by creating the stories in a sandbox tray with my great-aunt Lydia teaching us, dropped into my awareness. The verses were always short and simple ... for a child to learn. "Ask in my Name and you will receive ..." came into my heart.

My heart felt like it was breaking open, even while pleading. "Show me what to do" formed as a response in my awareness to the invitation to "Ask ..." And then, as if time had returned, I remembered that I was at Unity Village for an appointment, and if I didn't get there, I would be late.

A short time later, in another room, I was sitting with the person who had asked me to come. I knew him from a time when my husband had tried out in a church in the Northwest, and he had since come to work with the Association of Unity Churches at the world headquarters. We briefly talked before diving into what we both knew to be the question.

And then ... the numinous simply descended. That's one way that I would describe it now, even though I wouldn't have known that then. Now, I recognize it as a very rare Voice and Light experience. Suddenly the light began to change in the room. I heard a voice ... I thought, with my human mind, that it must be the person with whom I was sitting in the room. He later told me it wasn't. The voice simply asked: "If you could do anything in the world, what would you do?" Tears began filling my now closed eyes and then flowing down my cheek as I heard myself say the words, "I would be a minister."

And then the light changed again. I heard the voice of the person with whom I was meeting. He said in a somewhat excited voice, "If you really mean that ..." as he explained that deadlines were approaching for applications to ministerial school. He simply started directing me as to what to do, the next immediate steps that would redirect my life.

My human mind had never ever even thought about being a minister. That was what my husband did. Maybe we would do something together where my background and doctoral degree in education would be complementary. Yet all of my plans seemed to just simply dissolve into a greater knowing that came from beyond my rational mind.

I simply followed—moment by moment at times. I waited for and then followed the next points of light that came. I asked for them when I needed them. I followed them when they came. It became my spiritual practice, one that I still follow and teach. It was one of my first connections with radical trust and ultimately radical love.

Love has many faces in our lives. It shows up in so many ways, often with interesting and strange disguises. What has emerged, for me, is a radical surrender. It does, however, seem to take different lengths of time as it morphs into its expressions of "sometimes love, sometimes sorrow" in its exquisite journey of love without an opposite.

Ultimately, two or three years later, the marriage ended. Yet, for me, the love never ended. The dissolve of the breaking heart became the heart that was broken open, opening me to the next platforms, still then invisible, in this amazing journey of love.

## Practice: Bringing Your Life into the Curriculum

What have been moments in time that changed your life? How have they surprised you? How have they shifted and morphed? Can you see them now in new ways, through the eyes of love without an opposite?

Write for ten minutes maybe, perhaps for an hour. I love writing for one hour. For me it represents the Power of One, an other-worldly kind of connection.

Practice listening for the whispers, the knowing that comes from beyond our rational minds. Yours will be different from mine. Go beyond expectations …

Scribe what comes, without judging it, without editing it. If only silence comes, just sit. It will seem, perhaps, to come as a thought. Just scribe it. Let it come.

# CHAPTER 3

## *The Key to Everything*

WE SIT IN various classrooms in our lives; some of them even look like classrooms. Others look like ordinary other kinds of places. We hear voices in those settings. Sometimes we recognize, even honor and delight in, the voices we hear. Other times we don't. Occasionally, we call them teachers. Some have had formal roles; others have had informal roles.

Remembering clearly what we learned and who the teacher was may be more rare. Then, maybe once or perhaps a few times in a lifetime, time may stand still. Timelessness seems to penetrate into time. Words are spoken that imprint upon our hearts and minds. Sometimes they take us to new levels of recognition, perhaps of love or knowing that brings wonder, even awe.

Such a moment came in the first six weeks of my being in seminary at Unity School of Christianity. The class was Metaphysics I, and the day's topic was the story of creation found in the first chapter of Genesis in the Bible. Marvin Anderson was the teacher, a sort of radical revolutionary among Unity ministers.

"This is the key to everything," he said, "and we don't understand it yet." He then began to elaborate on the difference between what he called involution found in Genesis 1 and evolution, which he said was found in the rest of the Bible. He was taking us into the mystery, and he forewarned us … it was not about our necessarily understanding. I was fascinated with his charisma, with his passion.

And then I felt a shift. I felt myself transfixed, pierced by the words, held motionless in time. I knew, somehow, that this would be the work of the rest of my life. It was as if I was being given a life assignment. It was known that I could not understand it … yet. I told no one—not Marvin, not anyone. Who would I tell? It would sound crazy. Yet … there was a total knowing.

The pieces of that moment in time, the revelations of that knowing, have come over the three decades since. They still continue.

Involution is the descent of the Holy Spirit, the descent of the dove that artists have depicted. It is the living flame of love, the always already present known by mystics and poets. It is timeless, changeless, transcendent. And yet, it comes upon us, penetrating our souls, our hearts, our minds, our physical being. It ignites within us a yearning to know, to remember.

The ascent of the soul is felt in our heart as love. It is beyond human knowing. It doesn't make sense to us always, yet we want to know it more. It knows the impulse of its own becoming. It yearns for oneness, for union. Even though the world knows it not, we search for it, we seek it, yearn to find it.

At that moment in time in 1985, I could not have written these words. I had no way of even understanding them. I knew the creation story from my childhood. This was not that. My family, most of my friends, would not understand it. Somehow I had shifted out of a paradigm of awareness that included even a lot of my education. I was in between ... the unknowing would reveal itself in time.

What I know now is that my mind was dissolving into my heart, into a heart mind that would emerge in cosmic vastness. Mystics and map makers of consciousness have tried at times to describe the mysteries that are beyond the rational mind. Often the words are veiled; there is somehow a knowing that this can only be understood by "those who have the ears to hear, those who have the eyes to see ..."

And yet when the lightning bolt happens. When the thunder sounds, there is a knowing that does not require understanding. It begins with a love that changes everything and is forever.

## Practice: Bringing Your Life into the Curriculum

Give yourself the gift of just sitting in the silence, just being in your heart ... Feel your breath, breathing in with the awareness of "I Am," breathing out with the Awareness of "that" ... I Am That I am ...

Let the words dissolve as your heart feels them and then gives them out into the world ... Feel the pause points where awareness simply drops in from beyond the human mind. Open to revelation. Scribe it perhaps, or you may not remember it ...

What settings have been your classrooms? What voices did you hear? Who were the teachers in their formal or informal roles? What words imprinted in your awareness?

Have you felt shifts, moments when you felt transfixed, pierced by words? Have you experienced a glimpse, an awareness of a life assignment? How have you searched for it, yearned for it? How has it revealed itself over time?

What have you had no way of understanding? Have you known the in-between times, between the known and the unknowing?

Choose whatever questions light up or attract you and see if some of the mystery will come into words from beyond your human mind.

# CHAPTER 4

## *Living a Life of Ceaseless Discovery*

THE GUIDING WORDS *living a life of ceaseless discovery* are from A. H. Almaas. Speaking them and seeing them, I feel their vibration in the very core of my being. A gentle smile of recognition comes as I realize, "This vibration is working me, not the other way around."

There is a deep breath and a sigh. So simple and yet so complex. And all of the thoughts then just fade back into nothingness. Ceaselessly discovering, ceaselessly I Am That always already.

One of the ever reoccurring discoveries is the dance of my inner knower with the brilliant, even dazzling, outer teachers who simply show up along the way. So many significant pieces have been placed in this uniquely beautiful tapestry, this thousand-piece puzzle called living a life. There are so many exquisite pieces in this unity of oneness.

The seven days of creation seemed so simple in my childhood picture books filled with cosmic sky and earthly wonder. And now there have been more than seven decades of seeding the multicolored hues in this unique flowering garden of wonders.

The book *Spectrum of Consciousness* was a cosmic comet for me, the imprint of Ken Wilber, in the late 1980s to my questing heart and mind. States and stages began to do a slow waltz with my unfolding awareness of what would become for me the Codes of Co-Creation.

Other beloved teachers also showed up, often in surprising and unplanned ways, not orchestrated ways, as the seeds began their divinely timed process of ripening in my own garden amidst the flames. Andrew Harvey gave me those words. Their awareness ignited the way of passion in my heart.

Andrew and I were walking slowly through the garden on one of his multiple times of coming to Unity of Tustin to teach, this sacred place that was emerging in my heart and mind. Suddenly he stopped at the second garden site symbolizing faith and radical trust. Words began to almost excitedly flow …

"Oh, Marj, I just got the title of your book. It's *A Garden amidst the Flames.*" And then his eyes closed as I felt him descend into another place, his poet heart. More words flowed from his illumined being.

*"O Marvel! a garden amidst the flames. My heart has become capable of every form … I follow the religion of Love, that is my religion and my faith."* He told me it was from Ibn 'Arabi, a twelfth-century mystic and poet. I still have the scrap of paper on which he scribbled the title and handed it to me.

Significance, for me, can often come in threes. It is as if elements of Trinity are giving themselves. More master teachers were to become part of the structure that would be present-time dimensions of the Codes of Co-Creation.

The next amazing players in this cosmic unfolding would give more of the complexities of form. It came over multiple experiences in time as the light revealed itself, especially in spiral dynamics and the work of Dr. Don Beck. And then with silent meditation retreats, the double spiral of Thomas Keating came.

Often as new facets of each of the themes began to play, more master musicians simply came into the orchestra, bringing more brilliance of meaning. The incredible map of consciousness of Dr. David Hawkins, the MAP profiles of Susanne Cook-Greuter and the STAGES Inventory of Terri O'Fallon became part of the vastness of the colors of the rainbow now in my cosmic sky. Research and mysticism were coming together in what was happening in my twentieth- and twenty-first-century world.

## Practice: Bringing Your Life into the Curriculum

As you simply sit in the silence, allow yourself to just feel the breath, breathing in and out of your cosmic sky.

Your journey has been amazing in its own exquisitely unique way. Just take a moment and let it come in, with awareness that holds no judgment of what you or others might call right or wrong. Just be in awareness of the magnificence of what is.

How has the dance of people and places shown up for you? Feel it in your heart. Let it tell you. Can you experience the imprints of moments of cosmic comets and beloved teachers, some of whom may have shown up as a surprise in your own garden amidst the flames?

What perhaps began with a simple meaning and then began to show you its complexity of forms? Stay in your heart, where the field of love is pure.

Are there symbols that hold deep meaning that perhaps only you know?

Or make up your own questions. The knower within you knows them …

Scribing may be a way to bring the invisible meanings into the visible. I invite you to simply see what comes. If nothing comes, you could simply start with "I am experiencing nothingness, no-thing-ness." Then listen for the whispers that will follow, sometimes even days or weeks later.

# Code 1
## *Let There Be Light*

Site 1: Before "Let There Be Light"—Darkness and Void

# CHAPTER 5

## *Before "Let There Be Light"*

Do you know what was before "Let there be light"? If we don't, we are missing a very significant piece, a platform from which all of creation happens. And if the Codes of Co-Creation really are the key to everything, well ... we need to know the answer to that question.

When I use the Bible as my link, or sometimes as an oracle, to the mystery, what I know is there is a state of being that allows me to enter and decode the mystery. The silence is one of the ways of accessing that state. There are also others. All of them invite us to align our heart and mind, really align with That.

My way, most often, is to sit in the silence, feel my heart, let my mind dissolve as I breathe slowly and deeply, feel and know it. I listen for the whispers that drop in. They begin to download from realms beyond my human mind. I know it comes through the veils of the mystery. I call it mystical knowing.

If the first chapter of Genesis is a divine template, can it become a template for our lives? For me it has been, for more than three decades. Before that, I had never thought of it that way. I had never tested it. I had never followed the map to invoke the promises. And I would love to invite you to join me in the taste, the sweetness of what it offers.

Here are the very important words found in the first chapter of Genesis, the very first book in the Bible: "In the beginning God created the heavens and the earth. The earth was without form, and void; and darkness was on the face of the deep. And the Spirit of God was hovering over the face of the waters" (Genesis 1:1–2).

Without form, void, darkness, Spirit hovering ... So many times I had heard or read about the creation story in the first forty years of my life! How did I miss noticing *that*? That which was before the words "Let there be light." It always felt to me that it started with "Let there be light."

It would have explained so much that I couldn't understand. Words like *void* and *darkness* ... I didn't even know or remember they were there. But I had felt them. I knew them other ways ... before my mind knew.

The word *shy* comes when I think of myself as a child. I was a quiet and happy little girl who deeply loved her daddy. Yet I dissolved into that void and darkness at the age of eleven when my daddy died, very unexpectedly, at the age of thirty-nine. Has that been part of a cosmic imprint that I would feel unconsciously and sometimes even consciously?

Later, I would know it as feelings of loss that felt like abandonment. Of course, it was not his fault that he left or that I felt so alone. And my auto-responder feeling is still, to this day, to disappear, to dissolve in the darkness and the void when I feel a kind of what I call abandonment and loss.

Was there something more for me to know about this mystery of the void? Was it part of my yearning, leading me in a quest that would include religions of the world and spiritual teachers? And then I heard the word *void*, and it seemed as if for the first time … It is profoundly known, beyond words, in Buddhism, this deep vastness of the void.

Now the experience of "the face of the deep" is one of the faces of love in my life. This journey has taken me so far. Now I know the void as the source of all creation.

Heaven and earth, I now know not just in the physical, although I love it in the physical. Gazing into the cosmic sky connects me with the vastness of the invisible somehow. And I also know heaven and earth as realms within my own consciousness, my own being. I know the connection between Father Sky and Mother Earth. I feel the bridge and the comfort of the union.

In my inner awareness, heaven transcends yet includes earth. My divine awareness honors my human feelings and understanding. This brings also a knowing of multiple realities existing simultaneously. It has been so comforting, gently holding me, as I have experienced the passing through the veils of my son and of my beloved. Multiple realities existing simultaneously … Forever love is very real when one knows both realms.

Is this all part of the gifts of this amazing mystery? Translation happens, and meaning flows. *And the spirit of love was hovering over the face of the waters …* Somehow, in this unfolding, the words God and love have become synonyms.

"Then God said, 'Let there be light' and there was light. And God saw the light, that it was good; and God divided the light from the darkness. God called the light Day, and the darkness Night. So the evening and the morning were the first day" (Genesis 1:3–5).

Oh, my God … the invoking of light comes *after* the void and the darkness.

## Practice: Bringing Your Life into the Curriculum

The creation story unfolds with a template of seven. For me, this is part of the mystery. In the ancient scripture, it is called days. In my deep exploring, I have found miracles of revelation in looking at this template of seven-year cycles.

Sketch out a template of seven-year cycles in your life. We will come back to it from time to time. You will keep it where you can see it and refer to it. You will add things to it as you think of them, as they come back to you.

Begin with the years from zero to seven. You'll notice that this includes time in the womb. I love to work with it this way:

| | | |
|---|---|---|
| 0–7 | 7–14 | 14–21 |
| 21–28 | 28–35 | 35–42 |
| 42–49 | 49–56 | 56–63 |
| 63–70 | 70–77 | 77–84 |
| 84–91 | 91–98 | 98–beyond |

You'll notice we are approaching one hundred, a number of sacred meaning for me, representing the Power of One going into infinity! You will find out that we will also be working with future time that is part of the Now.

What you will begin to work with will be these cycles as they are interrelated to the stages of creation. You will find more mystery. Within each stage of each of the seven years is the code of the seven stages. The microcosm is in the macrocosm in each of the stages. But that's too complex for now!

To begin with, you will just create the template. What you will find is that the template will begin revealing itself, even before we go into some of our dialogues about the seven stages of co-creation.

You may feel it happening even as you look at the template. Significant people, events, and moments in time will just drop in. Jot down names, events, words in the blank spaces. You are going to find out this is really a fun and beautiful thing!

I am so looking forward to sharing this journey with you.

# CHAPTER 6

## *Do We See It?*

JUNE 6 WAS an important day for me. It was the day of my son's birth. I was only twenty years old, almost a child myself! Did I know that we would only have forty-six years together, including the time that I carried him in the womb with such anticipation?

It was also the birthday of the son of my beloved, my first love when we were in our teens. Our experience of first love for each of us cycled in time, both of us marrying others, both of our sons being born on June 6, one year apart, both of them passing through the veils within weeks of each other when they were both in their forties.

Could we have known that we would find all of that out when we were in our seventies? Did it have meaning beyond the appearances in time? When he found me again in our seventies, he was surprised and curious to find that I was a minister. Religion had never really been a part of his life. Spirituality was simply natural.

He asked me so many questions ... deep questions. I answered in sometimes-long e-mails, sometimes telephone conversations. He was the one who said, "You must write." My response was, "The only reason I write is because you ask me questions."

He asked if I would write if he gave me questions. I said, "Yes."

Four questions came with one condition, that I would promise to write on them: Who am I? Who are you? Who are we? What is our purpose?

I began to write long responses. The third question was just completed ...

It was open on his computer. He had read it several times on the day that I drove one hundred miles to his home in the desert because he was not answering his phone. I knew something was wrong. He had passed through the veils. I found him in his recliner. Could we have known we only had three years left in the physical together?

Let's go back and reread, see again, the passages from Genesis that we have been considering. We may see things that didn't register before. Sometimes it is not for our human minds to know or to understand the vastness, the complexities of light and dark, or the knowing of the good. Yet we can know eternal love ...

Have you ever considered letting yourself hear the mystery? Have you even listened in the silence? Have you ever entered the words of sacred scripture as the key to everything? I've found it to be one of the great gifts of my life. It may take revisiting many times. Still, for me, it continues to unfold, even now as I write:

God saw the light, that *it was good* ...

First came the invoking of the light, "Let there be light." Then God saw the light and saw that it was good. I find it curious that in my Bible, *it was good* is in italics and in the past tense. It is as if it is emphasized in a different way, perhaps indicating a different way of seeing, maybe taking time.

If events in our lives feel like "darkness on the face of the waters," we can know, perhaps, that it is part of a greater process. We can open and breathe into the space within us, even though it feels unknown, even heartbreaking or empty.

We can call forth, invoke the light from that within us that knows the heavens and the earth, even though it seems impossible to know in this moment in time. The invisible is there, as well as the visible experience; we just can't see it or perhaps even feel it.

It seems there are three parts, a sort of trinity. It includes saying it, invoking it, perhaps only in our thoughts if we can't feel the way to say it out loud. Then it includes seeing it and knowing it was good. That may be the hard one; at least it has been for me. When my whiteboard has been erased, it's hard to know it as good. It feels devastating sometimes when we experience the dissolve.

What I've noticed is that I can't always do all three of these in the moment something is occurring. Perhaps that is one of the realities of time. Things get triggered; it just seems to happen. It's a feeling like being blindsided, hurt, sad, even mad.

A psychologist once told me that there are basic feelings, including sad, mad, and glad. I like the way the words rhyme; it makes them easy to remember. Often I feel glad and happy; that's delightful and easy for me. Yet interestingly, even the good of those kinds of moments can change.

And then we can notice that there are two phases, at least, to this whole process. They are natural parts that we just take for granted as simply what is. There is day and night, light and dark, both/and, both part of a natural whole. It's simple when we think of day and night. It's not so simple when we think of joy and sorrow.

Yet we begin to see that there is a cosmic or otherworldly process that somehow divides the light from the darkness. Recognition can come that we are part of it if we open into that transcendent part of ourselves, our higher power, ask for and see the light, even in the invisible, and know that it was good.

Sometimes I have to go to the timelessness, to the forever love, to the unchanging, to know good when I am feeling so lost, alone, and not knowing what to do. My hardest initiation into that kind of lost-ness has been death. It simply has taken me time to find my new level of the unfolding good.

A significant key seems to be hidden in these few words: invoking (asking), seeing (even in the dark), and knowing it was good (even as you are gentle with yourself, breathe into it and give yourself time). All three are part of the spiraling process, of the higher and deeper, of the creation of that which is to come.

It may seem like we've spent a huge amount of time in the beginning, in this first piece of our potential journey, this first day, this first stage. The feeling may be that nothing is happening, that there has to be more. We may get restless and want to jump ahead, skip stuff, or even check out.

The first phases of our journey together will be in the invisible. This was only the first stage. There are two more stages in the invisible for us if we are to shift to knowing the changeless, the eternal that is part of our soul's plan, our own unique destiny path that is part of the whole.

At the core of every cell of our being is light. It is in us, and it is all around us. It is in people who are part of our lives, in every experience of our lives. And it is in every experience of the world. Our human minds can't wrap themselves around that. It is not meant to be understood by the human mind.

In our experience of separation, we often don't understand it consciously. Yet we can know the cycles of light and dark as part of the vastness that is good.

For nineteen years during the time of my role as senior minister at Unity of Tustin, every Sunday morning started with the congregation singing, *"Surely the presence of the Lord is in this place. I can feel its power and its grace."* My opening prayer always began, "Oh, Beloved One, Holy Spirit … Come upon us … Come … Holy Spirit."

On the day, now nearly twelve years ago, when my son collapsed on a weekend trip, the imprint of the words "Come, Holy Spirit" was what I remember speaking after I ran to him and held him in my arms, not realizing that he was passing through the veils. The full coffee cup that he was bringing to me had shattered as it fell onto the concrete patio. It had jolted me from looking out over a lake. Moments of serenity changed into shock and not knowing.

Yet what I know now, in the moments of surprise that seem to change everything, is that there is an Always Already realm where there is another way of knowing. We can access it, even when we don't understand it.

There's a piece of paper sitting next to my computer that I glance at often. I don't remember where the words came from … "I got on the wheel and went to the end … And the funny thing is … at the end, there was another beginning …"

## Practice: Bringing Your Life into the Curriculum

If you created the template to be filled in, now you can begin to fill it in more. You may actually want to create a separate sheet, or even pages, for each stage or theme. It will be up to you how much you do, how willing you are to take the deep dives.

If you decide to do it, it will be like climbing up a ladder to the platform that will give you a profound glimpse of awareness into your unique soul destiny. You may have glimpses of why's that perhaps you have never understood. It may even give you glimpses into future time that you will begin to see and know.

## Expand the Practice:
## Dividing the Light from the Darkness

I have found it useful as I've done my own exploring to simply fold a piece of paper in half vertically. Write Light in one column and Darkness in the second.

What I love doing, from the witness state that sees with awareness beyond judgment of right and wrong, is to just jot down words or phrases that come. They may be events, people, circumstances, settings, places, whatever comes.

I've found it most useful to give myself room to add to it later, leaving blank space. The use of the template of seven-year cycles has been very meaningful for me.

Jesus taught in parables. There was a profound reason for this. Using parables, many levels of teaching are available in the form of one simple story. It will all depend on having the ears to hear, the eyes to see. So it will be with you.

I'm also aware of what one of my seminary teachers once said. Ed Rabel was an amazing teacher of the mysteries in the teachings of Jesus. He said: "Jesus came back from the future."

There are multiple realities existing simultaneously. As we experience our journey, moving through states and stages, moving into vaster realms of living consciously, we will begin to see future with vertical awareness as a reality that is always already present.

It will be different from seeing future as part of the dimension of horizontal time that includes past, present, and future. The now can be an intersection between these two ways of seeing.

The practice of bringing your life into the curriculum is a very powerful practice, one of the most powerful that I know. Do not underestimate it or skip over its value. Without it, what you get is cognitive knowledge, which is good but not as transforming. What you do with these invitations will be entirely up to you. This is an invitation to experiential learning. You will find its value and its vastness, or maybe not.

If you do, you will begin to see that your very own life is not just a story; it is a parable. It is a sacred love story, perhaps being known or told for future time.

# CHAPTER 7

# *The In-Between Times*

THERE ARE LINES that I love from an old song, "All the Way," by Frank Sinatra. One phrase especially pops into my awareness: *"Through the good or lean years, and for all the in-between years ..."*

Other phrases are also important to me. They also come: *"Who knows where the road will lead us? Only a fool would say. But if you'll let me love you, it's for sure I'm gonna love you all the way ..."*

I hear those simple words now, like cosmic music of knowing and unknowing. Sometimes, for me, simple music that I've loved in my life is like a mantra. It is a simple and deep way of experiencing life. I can't figure it out, even though I try. There are cycles of good and lean times, as well as in-between times.

And there is a love that, if I recognize it, is always with me, all the way. I call it forever love. I know that love shows up in human form as well as invisible form. Both are sometimes, rarely perhaps, in the same package. That will include relationships, work as pilgrimage, nature, and more.

The meditation gardens at Unity of Tustin, for me, are one of those experiences in time that are timeless. They are symbolic of all of the stages of our entire lives. And they are also about collective consciousness, the story of humankind.

Each site in the garden can be applied to the individual events of our unfolding journey. It is also applicable to the whole story, where we are in awareness, as a community, a country, a planet. It is the microcosm, and it is the macrocosm. And it is everything in between. It is our life alone, and it is our life in relationship.

In this experience of putting together all of the pieces of our thousand-piece puzzle, we have the puzzle box with all of the individual pieces; it's called our life. Yet somehow the cover picture of what it will finally look like got lost.

Finding our way to put the pieces together takes time, even though there are clues that we figure out. We may sort out the pieces that are easy first, like ones with straight edges that are indicators they are potential borders of our particular puzzle. We may also look for different colors that sort of match up. We look for shades, even perhaps of forms that are to come.

What I've noticed is that the whole picture emerges in stages, sort of clusters of pieces sometimes of the whole. I've taken some of the pieces out and laid them on the side as I've looked at ways to put others together. A picture begins to reveal itself. Sometimes other people will help me put the puzzle together.

Another symbol that has had immense meaning for me is the spiral. There is a connecting path that seems to move horizontally in ascending and descending circles. Yet it is clear that the view of the whole includes seeing vertically. It's the way to see all the way.

In the garden at Unity of Tustin, there is a point on the path in between the first and the second stage. It was developed by the prayer chaplains so they could have a place to pray with people. The whole journey is depicted in the art of the stepping-stones that lead to the bench where people can sit in prayer. The symbols on each of the stepping-stones are of the seven chakras.

As we move in the experience of our lives unfolding, it is like the puzzle and the spiral dancing! Often we are moving to different points or levels on the spiral, and we are trying to put in the pieces that belong there. Sometimes we are in stages. We've earned them, and they seem to last for a while. Sometimes we are in states that come and go. They come and then seem to disappear. We may think we had it and then lost it. Yet we have a center of gravity to which we seem to return.

Each of the stepping-stones in the garden site is a glimpse of one of those stages. There are no details. It's a bit like walking into a puzzle store and seeing that there are different puzzles available. Some will appeal to us now; others won't ... yet they may later. There is no rush to get all of the puzzles. Yet could it be, somehow, that at one point we will see that there is an overall theme or knowing?

An additional complexity may show up in our lives when we try to nail it down, control it. We want to feel safe and secure; it's important and natural. Yet that point that we think we can stand on is moving.

It's a spiral, as well as a puzzle, and there is an impulse that is yearning for us to go higher and deeper. We feel it, yearning for us ... and we feel that yearning within us that responds. It's about transcending what we thought we knew, integrating more, even while including the good, the true, and the beautiful of all that we have experienced.

The invitation is to a vaster knowing. It will feel like integrating more and more, perhaps like growing up. And simultaneously, sometimes without knowing it, we are also waking up to an invisible inner something that we feel almost as if we have always known it.

The complexity will ultimately dissolve into a simplicity that is like … love. That's my word for what I experience. Your word could be peace or joy. Yet it is different from love, or peace, or joy that we've previously known. This is something that has no opposite. It just is. And it includes the world we know, as it is. It's sort of a strange land. In the beginning, we may feel like a stranger in it. You'll know your word when it happens.

It is like the rainbow. The colors are spectacular, and you don't have to create them. You can't take one color out; they are all part of the whole. And yet there are different colors; each is part of the beauty. Sometimes there is also a double rainbow, in rare moments, perhaps after some kind of unusual storm or rain that seems to make everything fresh and clear.

What seems important to sort of get if you stop to sit on the bench at this place in the garden is that things and perceptions from one level or color or stage of our lives have to show up in their own colors. And even though we see the rainbow clearly, we can't actually keep it … except perhaps as a sacred and precious knowing.

The in-between times are also there. Often things and perceptions from one level or stage of our lives have to dissolve in order to open into what is coming. It is a natural part of making way, creating the space, for things that are part of our future time, part of our soul's plan, part of our destiny path. There are beginnings and endings in the vastness of cosmic and human experience, as all one.

## Practice: Bringing Your Life into the Curriculum

In times of trouble, in times of confusion or sorrow, this place in cosmic knowing can be a very comforting "bridge over troubled waters."

It gives you time to sit in the quiet, to breathe, to feel like you are being held in the arms of the invisible. You don't have to understand it or even figure out what to do. It will hold you when you don't know the way.

The engaging with your individual invisible will be strengthened by your connecting with this invisible vastness. Find your places for this. It may be in nature; it may be a sacred place that you are guided to. It may be a person who shows up, like an angel in a human disguise. This is a time to be gentle with yourself.

Take some time to become aware of this always already presence that has been there in your life, sometimes in strange or surprising disguises. Write about it, if you are willing. It might help other people some day, and it will help you today, if you are in one of those spaces of troubled waters or unknowing.

Look at the template of your life with the spaces that still have blank space, where words have not been written. See if certain moments of darkness had some of these moments. Be aware of moments of light coming in as surprise or revelation.

See if you can recognize how experiences of creating, maintaining, and dissolving have been part of one whole at various stages in your life.

# CHAPTER 8

## *Spectrums of Rainbows*

I woke up seeing it—spectrums of rainbows. Then I realized they were coming to me all day yesterday. Now it's clear; it is all spectrums of consciousness. It's only that I get it in smaller pieces that I can sort of handle. Even so, I may not notice. I may not put the pieces together.

*The Spectrum of Consciousness,* by Ken Wilber, came to me in 1988 when I was the minister at Unity of Walnut Creek, California. I gave a series of talks on it and taught classes midweek to bring people's lives into the experience. *No Boundary,* also by Ken Wilber, a simple guide interrelating types of therapies to consciousness, along with Spectrum, was blasting my mind open into a vastness that was bringing together, making sense of, so much of my life.

The macrocosm is in the microcosm; the whole is in the parts. It's holographic. There are so many ways to say it. A flash of a memory, way before, of seeing a movie called *The Powers of 10* comes in. The universe and the galaxies are in every cell of our body.

And so it is with the rainbow in all of its magnificent beauty, visible and invisible, depending on the reflections of light. There is a rainbow, the full spectrum, within every experience, setting, and person, including ourselves, within every stage, every moment of our lives.

It is there, still and moving, unconscious and conscious, always. Sometimes we see, and other times we don't. It's quite mind blowing to get a glimpse of it, even while realizing you've always known it, somehow, in your heart.

Every stage of our lives has all of the colors, all different vibrations of light, seen and unseen. As we grow in awareness, the colors repeat themselves in different density of vibration, giving us gifts of new perspectives, new perceptions going beyond what was before. It's like higher octaves of the same note!

The amazing thing, for me, is that all of the good, the true, and the beautiful are there at the core, always already, in its process of flowering. Life lessons come and go, emerge and dissolve, as we play our parts in this movie that we think is real.

A dear friend Betsy, who was a member of the congregation in Walnut Creek, gave me a beautiful crystal as I sat with her when she was in the process of dying. She handed me the crystal and told me it had hung in her window for years. Now she wanted me to have its beauty.

Now, more than two decades later, it still hangs in my window on transparent threads. Yesterday in the late-afternoon sun, the spectrum of light was dancing all across the opposite living room wall. It was dazzling, these multiple rainbow spectrums dancing in a gentle breeze.

I was sitting in the living room with three angels in my life. Two of them know their angel-ness in my life vividly. One of them is still wondering. One who knows is John Welshons, the author of *Awakening from Grief.* The other is beautiful Fabienne. We were laughing about how the universe had arranged for John to show up on my doorstep when I was immersed in grief, not knowing how to transcend and include it.

Our conversation moves through all of the shades of playful and deep. There are insights of joy, sorrow, delight, and confusion that become part of the unfolding dialogue. It is truly an amazing journey in which we have somehow found ourselves and each other.

All of the colors are there, appearing and dissolving in this sometimes strange and magnificent dance, this moment in time. Suddenly I feel it, this overwhelming gratitude and a deep love that moves through me, bringing tears to my eyes. And then a soft smile comes as I stand and walk to the door with John to say good-bye one more time.

## Practice: Bringing Your Life into the Curriculum

Choose a slice of time in your life, maybe a day, two or three weeks, perhaps more. See it as part of the dancing colors of the spectrum of the rainbow. I love to find it in the seemingly ordinary moments. Somehow, it will show you.

Sometimes it will come in a dream and then will be present as you come into waking consciousness. Our dream symbols can give us deep and delightful insight into our unfolding life, even cosmic journey. They will include the dazzling darkness, the dark that is filled with invisible light. Spectrums of dark and light are a natural part of the dance of day and night.

How have these spectrums of rainbows shown up in your life? Don't try to figure it out with your mind. This is more an experience of revelation, and it is of the heart, of the soul. If you are willing to write, just make that commitment, maybe for ten minutes, maybe for an hour, and see what comes. You won't know what it has to tell you until you start writing.

How has awareness revealed itself over time? How have the glimpses come? How did they weave themselves together, these moments of insight? Write from your heart, from your soul. Let it come from beyond your rational mind.

And see the way that your rational mind will support it, delight in it, and perhaps at times discount or argue with it. When we don't judge it, we find the play in it. We are complex and beautiful beings of light.

# Code 2

## *Radical Trust and Faith*

Site 2: Water Wall
Separating the Waters Above from the Waters Below

# CHAPTER 9

## *Invisible Dimensions of the Soul*

How do we access the invisible dimensions of our soul? Is it even possible for us, or does it simply come upon us, into our awareness, in moments of grace? What is the soul, and how do we even know it's there? There are so many questions and seemingly no way to prove it. Until it happens … something so clear … and then the questions dissolve as answers begin to come.

The second code of radical trust and faith has a somewhat mysterious feeling. It seems as of an ancient knowing, strange to understand.

"Let there be a firmament in the midst of the waters, and let it divide the waters from the waters." The voice of God is speaking again. Is it an inner voice, an outer voice, in the world, not of the world? And what does "a firmament" mean?

Then this ancient text says the firmament is made. The waters that *were* under the firmament are divided from the waters that *were* above the firmament. I notice the "were" two times is in italics in my Bible. It seems like more mystery. Why just these words?

Then, another astounding realization: "And God called the firmament Heaven. So the evening and the morning were the second day" (Genesis 1: 6–8).

My astounding wonder was: what happened to earth? I don't think that I'd ever noticed that both weren't mentioned here, not in all the years that I've taught this. I looked more closely without knowing it and opened to my mind dissolving into a greater awareness.

Such intriguing clues are in these codes that go back thousands of years. Is there a way to bring all of this, with our contemporary ways of knowledge and science, into our now awareness? Can we align who we know ourselves to be now with this ancient text? Does it make any sense after thousands of years?

Charles Fillmore, the cofounder of Unity, wrote a book called *Mysteries of Genesis*. Actually, he gave talks; they were transcribed, and the book came from them. He focuses on "a firmament," and ultimately, in Unity, it has become part of the foundation of affirmative prayer. It is part of Silent Unity, the ministry of prayer, known worldwide.

Is this about a way of thinking, and even feeling, a way of believing and trusting? And if it is, if we let it become part of our lives, what happens? Is it a way of being that changes us, even possibly changes our world?

I notice that, for me, this is not about heavy-handed rule making. It is a voice speaking that ancient scripture calls God. Could this voice now be like an inner voice that is natural and a very early part of creation when it is still invisible?

It seems there is a dividing place between the positive and the negative. Could this be part of the mystery of kinesiology, or the research of Dr. David Hawkins and his life work, including *Power*

*Vs. Force* and ending with *Letting Go*? Is it the shift occurring at level 200 on the map of consciousness that tracks changes in energy from destructive to life affirming?

Are there other monumental leaps that occur in us and in humankind as a whole—shifts we are still moving toward in consciousness? Could another monumental shift be at the level of 500, at love and above, on the map of consciousness?

The monumental leap phenomena is researched, written, and taught in the work of *Spiral Dynamics* with Dr. Don Beck. The spiral dynamics research is very extensive, and the work of Don Beck has had significant impact in the world.

It is also part of the *Integral Life* framework of Ken Wilber that has been so deeply studied, researched, and embraced by more and more people. Is this part of the tipping point of which Ken Wilber so brilliantly and passionately speaks, to which he has devoted his work and his life?

Clearly the questions come, often as the experience of answers come. For me, it has not happened suddenly but over three decades. Sometimes the answers have even come first, with the questions after, a reverse-order way. It feels like the 180-degree shift in perception that is found in the teachings of *A Course in Miracles*.

So much curiosity, so many questions. Radical trust and a faith beyond belief have also come to me in all of these years of life, study and teaching, of wandering as I wonder. It has been a quest and an odyssey that still continues. Time dissolves into timelessness. Curiosity is a powerful entry point in this odyssey.

And then my mind dissolves back into the astounding realization that I noticed in the beginning of this particular writing:

"And God called the firmament Heaven. So the evening and the morning were the second day" (Genesis 1:8).

The unconscious waters that *were* perceived as under and above are now simply called Heaven. Evening and morning are still there, different shades of light and color. I am seeing beautiful sunsets and sunrises as part of that color.

Somehow a monumental shift has occurred in the way I see. It goes beyond perceptions of the under and above. It is what I have called non-dual awareness. Could this be part of what mystics have called the dazzling darkness?

Another awareness comes to me, a teaching I learned from Thomas Keating. Every time we shift into a higher level of light in this amazing double spiral, it shines the light on a deeper level of darkness. The light is used to transform more darkness.

It feels very much like this has been part of the colors of my own consciousness, my own spiraling higher and deeper as I have evolved in stages of knowing. A tapestry of colors is revealing its hues, shades, and beauty.

## Practice: Bringing Your Life into the Curriculum

What have been your answers at different stages of your life? What has your process of questions looked like? Have your questions brought new answers? Do new answers transcend and include some of your previous values? What has the *include* looked like?

Has there been some dissolve with things that no longer feel of value to you? How have your values changed in different stages of your life? Do you still value the value of it at the stage where it showed up?

How do you see stages of development in your own life? Who have been the people who have been most significant for you in this process? Have there been significant books, places, teachings, or settings?

I'm noticing that as I wrote, there were a lot of questions! How would it impact what I wrote if I were to turn my questions into answers? How would I answer my own questions from perhaps another higher voice within me?

What are your answers now? Are they inspiring more questions or perhaps even more action? How has it worked for you?

# CHAPTER 10

## To What Are You Faithful?

THE BEAUTY OF faith and trust, for me, is that they don't change in the invisible. I know that as I breathe into my heart and let my human mind dissolve into That, I Am That. It is formless and changeless.

It can be another story when we get lost in the outer, the visible, and begin to expect what the outer scenario or person will do, how it or they will respond to our projected hope. There's a strange paradox here.

The imprint that is in my heart whispers: "Faith, hope and love, these three; but the greatest of these is love" (1 Corinthians 13:13).

As I look to see if I am remembering the words correctly, I find what comes before.

"For we know in part … But when that which is perfect has come, then that which is in part will be done away. When I was a child, I spoke as a child, understood as a child, I thought as a child; but when I became a man, I put away childish things" (1 Corinthians 13:9–11).

My mind takes notice of the word *man*. It's been part of a mind-set to shift to inclusive language for over thirty years now in my life. My higher mind has come to translate *man* to words that do not exclude my feminine body and being. I even have written "another word" under "man" in my Bible.

The word I wrote at some point, probably when I was teaching it, was *grown*, when I became grown. Now it might be something like *mature*. Yet it seems even beyond that. Maybe *whole*, when I became whole, or even *one*, when I became one with the One.

Then the whisper interrupts what it sees as less significant, probably mind-stuff:

"For now we see in a mirror, dimly, but then face to face. Now I know in part, but then I shall know just as I also am known" (1 Corinthians 13:12).

A flash of a memory comes, from years ago, in this multi-reality dialogue. I was aware that my second marriage was in some bumpy territory, dissolving somehow, and I desperately didn't want it to happen. My imprint from my childhood was that marriage was for life, until death do us part. My first marriage had ended. I didn't want that to happen to the second. Am I repeating myself? Is there purpose in that? Is this what occurs with deep imprints still healing?

One night, we were trying to communicate … and it just wasn't happening. I was feeling lost in something I didn't understand. Suddenly a more expansive consciousness, vaster yet silent, enveloped me. Silent words came as I looked at my husband: *you don't even know me*. The words were simply there, unspoken. Tears came, gentle, silent tears, a knowing of the unknowing.

I smile now as I remember myself then, barely in my forties, with my just-completed doctoral degree in education, including a focus in counseling, which seemed totally inadequate for what we were experiencing. It had to have been hard for him also, just out of seminary, finding his own way to stand on holy ground.

One of the conversations I remember between us had to do with just a word; it was the word *substance*. He was trying to tell me what substance was.

For me, it was something completely different. It was physical, or at least the material from which something is made. It could even mean material possessions. It could include stuff, even like ingredients for a cake. I was feeling exasperated, not angry but like it was hopeless. It was a prickly feeling.

He never told me that he was trying to describe what Charles Fillmore, the cofounder of Unity, called substance. Years later, I would use words like *essence*, concepts like the *ultimate reality* that underlies all outward manifestation and change. I would know and teach that "Faith is the Substance of things hoped for, the evidence of things not seen" (Hebrews 11:1).

There was too big a gap in our human awareness. And we didn't know it or know how to bridge it. We didn't know the substance, the essence that we both shared. We didn't have a way that we could see it and clearly communicate it.

We were simply in different countries, speaking different languages. Both were right for the country in which they existed. And we didn't manage to find the permeable boundaries.

Faith, hope, and love, these three ... and the greatest of these is love. Maybe this heartbreak in my life, when the divorce happened, was part of the igniting of what I now call the living flame of love in my heart.

Was this a stepping-stone of the heart that would take me to some future stepping-stones? Was this part of the light shining on the darkness that would bring the seemingly unceasing questions? Is that what lies above and below questions and answers as they spiral higher and deeper in this vastness that I now call the essence of the All That Is?

## Practice: Bringing Your Life into the Curriculum

What have been the heartbreaks and breakthrough experiences in your life? How has a vaster love been ignited?

This is not limited to personal relationships; it can include work, purpose, anything. Your heart will tell you.

Try applying it to all of these, maybe at different times of deep soul writing and scribing.

# CHAPTER 11

## Your Unique Gifts of Genius

WE NOW COME to one of the most important parts of this journey without distance. It's you and the unique gifts that no one has in the same way you do. It's the song of your soul that only you can play. It is in gifts of genius that you can have radical trust and radical faith.

You are already playing it at some level of vibration; you may just not be realizing it. It requires your saying yes, following the notes of the music that compose its song.

I was fascinated and felt awe when I recently heard Thomas Hübl, an amazing mystical teacher, say, "Genius people tap into future territory." There are two ways to talk about the future. One is as another point in time, not yet occurring, a horizontal kind of trajectory that has past, present, and future in sequence.

Another possibility is to know vertical awareness, to know there are multiple realities existing simultaneously. We can connect with our genius beyond our normal human perception. We open into, go beyond, and bring back fruits from a territory that we don't "know."

It usually will take development to see with vertical awareness. We can see only when we have the eyes to see, if we have the openness to receive. Until then, it doesn't exist. Yet we are infused with our future; it is always already present even though it is beyond our recognition.

Something in me absolutely lights up to hear these things. I've sensed it, known it, and often felt aligned with it for a lot of years. You may have also, at least to some extent. Especially when you hear it put into words, you may recognize it.

I didn't call it *gifts of genius* until a few years ago. It would have felt pretentious. Now it doesn't. At a time when I was raw enough, vulnerable and open enough, it was part of what called me. And then it showed me the way.

We are born with our unique and different gifts. They are imprinted in our very being, our soul's DNA. They are like star seed transmissions that call us, if we listen to the whispers of our soul's knowing. They show us gifts related to our destiny. They show up in different ways, sort of with disguises perhaps, at different or sometimes repeating times in our lives.

This is a good time to fill in more of the blank spaces on your creation story, the template you are sketching out in seven-year cycles. In coming from the invisible, our gifts of genius often start in simple ways and have many facets. Let me give you an ordinary example of how this works.

One of my early childhood memories is music. My father had a beautiful tenor voice and loved to sing. "When Irish Eyes Are Smiling" and "Danny Boy" were two of his favorites and, of course, mine. I learned to play for him to sing when I was five years old and started piano lessons. You may notice there are multiple imprints here. You have them also; you'll see them when you look!

The swivel-up, round piano stool that I sat on at the upright piano in the dining room of my childhood home in Boulder, Colorado, now sits in front of the mirror in the master bath of my Southern California home. I still feel the energy of it in the morning as I sit to do my hair.

The imprint is part of the music my soul has played through my entire life. I felt the yearning and became a harpist in my teens, playing "Liebestraum," "Dream of Love." It became a kind of signature. It played deeply in my soul, and now it goes around the world ending dialogues on www.LivingLovingLegacy.com.

There are hundreds of stories like this in your thousand-piece puzzle. The pieces are laid out on the table, upside down. We gradually turn them over, see the colors and shapes, see how they fit together and reveal the amazing picture of the ways our soul is guiding us and helping us create.

Some pieces will have to do with what you are drawn to, sometimes in mysterious ways. They may involve significant people or events that change your life. Seeds may ultimately grow. The beacon of these gifts of genius is guiding you. They will light up spaces of darkness and guide you to healing. You may recognize them in ways that you feel delight or are nourished. You feel them in your heart.

Symbols or traditions may come into your awareness with a spiritual kind of feeling that may or may not be related to any kind of God experience. It can happen in nature. It will impact choices you make, even significant choices like education or career, as well as deep and different kinds of relationships.

I've found my gifts of genius in learning, teaching, and facilitating. They are in beauty, family, and deep relationships. They are the beloved, found in treasured moments, cherished memories, in passion and in purpose. Love is my code word. When I recognize it, I know I'm aligned and in the flow of love's field.

They become gifts of a higher and different kind. They may be for a purpose greater than for just our personal self. Unique gifts will dance together and often will dance with the gifts of others so they may be offered to the world.

## Practice: Bringing Your Life into the Curriculum

You may have noticed that there is only one rather short story in this segment on your unique gifts of genius. When you write about your own life, it may seem like just a story. Part of you may have been told not to tell your story—too much ego, too personal, too … whatever.

What I want us to realize is that when we write or speak about our lives, our stories, from the field, the state of pure love, what happens is that we are seeing from an entirely different sphere. It is not ego; it is the field of a sacred love story.

Our personal stories hold the potential of becoming love embodied. One of the books that I love the most by Llewellyn Vaughan-Lee, a profound mystic, is *Fragments of a Love Story*. It is his own story written from his pure heart.

Constance Kellough, on our telesummit, www.Living LovingLegacy.com, talked about how she had assisted Eckhart Tolle as he wrote and self-published *The Power of Now*. She said they often have talked about how they see, in each of their lives, golden threads. At one point, the threads crossed, and it changed both of their lives. I call this intersections in time. I write about these. You can click on any name under any picture on the telesummit landing page. It's after each bio. And you can still listen to the dialogues.

Your practice for this segment of your exploration is to identify some of your own gifts of genius and some of your own golden threads.

People who know you, if they really know you, may see your gifts of genius more clearly than you do. They can tell you sometimes, if you ask them.

One of the things that I sometimes suggest is for you to ask at least three people. Tell them it is an assignment. Ask them to tell you what they see as your gifts of genius. Record what they say, if you can. Or they could write it down. And let them know this is not about weakness; this is helping you see, a gift of another kind!

Write now for at least ten minutes, maybe more. Just let it come. Put your pen on the blank sheet of paper. Let love show you what it wants to write.

How has it shown up over time in your life, perhaps beginning in childhood? Have you had blocks or obstacles that had to melt away? How have you experienced these gifts, as they eventually revealed themselves in your life, perhaps over and over in different or sometimes strange ways?

Can you now see it with vertical awareness? Can you realize that you may tap into future territory and that you can bring back gifts from beyond your current human-mind knowing?

# CHAPTER 12

## *Kissing the Darkness*

THERE'S A PLACE on the California coast south of Big Sur called Ragged Point. I found it first in the 1980s and have been drawn to return from time to time. It's beautiful; the cliffs are steep and rugged as they fall into the sea.

I knew I was feeling compelled to go back after spending a beautiful week in a silent meditation retreat with Adyashanti. It was at Asilomar, near Pacific Grove and the Restless Sea. It is not far north from where the Big Sur coastline starts. In the winter month of November, weather can be unpredictable. It can be stunningly beautiful, or rain and storms can come.

We headed south on Highway 1 in the midafternoon. The sun was shining through occasional white, fluffy clouds. Yet, even a third of the way into the distance, we could see the indicators. The clouds were showing shades of darkness. I chose to ignore them, and we forged ahead anyway. "Compelled" is not easily stoppable.

Several hours later, we had driven very slowly through dense fog, heavy rain, and occasional rockslides. It was a trip with none of the beautiful views available in the gray overcast skies and later darkness. We arrived at Ragged Point, very relieved to be there. There was a room available, for one night only.

In the gift shop the next morning, I found a slender book of love poems and art by Carolyn Mary Kleefeld and David Wayne Dunn. It was called *Kissing Darkness*. I was drawn to pick it up and open it. The titles of the poems were equally compelling as I scanned a few passages and felt its exquisite beauty before making it mine.

Leaving the bookstore, we were greeted by hundreds of butterflies, beautiful beyond description. They were headed north on their annual pilgrimage. In the glory of the morning, we also set out to retrace our drive in the dark, wanting to see the beauty and the majesty of the sheer cliffs rising out of the sea.

My heart yearned to see the Big Sur mountains dropping into the vastness of the blue Pacific. I wanted to see clearly what was not visible in the stormy and even treacherous night. I could go back with new eyes, dissolve my memory of the difficult night before.

I remembered the awe of another time, after rain, at Ragged Point. I had witnessed one of the most exquisite double rainbows I've ever seen. It was so breathtaking that it is still imprinted in my mind and heart.

Sometimes in our lives we have our ragged points, experiences and circumstances that are traversed with great difficulty, sorrow, or fear. They can come as a surprise, unplanned, out of the blue. Sometimes it is not totally a surprise, and we forge ahead anyway.

These times can begin with great love, joy, and anticipation that can absolutely light up our hearts, ignite our lives with beauty. And even in these moments, with the difficulty that ignites pain, the beauty can turn into darkness and unknowing.

Destiny paths will include both light and dark, often both joy and sorrow. And yet, if they are truly paths of destiny, perceived with the eyes of the soul, they may be the source of some of our greatest gifts of genius.

And it requires our going through the darkness, seeing beyond the duality of opposites into the vastness of the light that is always already there, beyond the cycles we are experiencing in time.

The gifts that emerge will not be ones we asked for necessarily, or anticipated as something we wanted. Yet, because we have done the journey, we know in every cell of our being what it takes to traverse the path. We will know how to guide others through. If we say yes to this call, we will be standing on holy ground.

Jesus called it, "You are the light of the world." In eastern spiritual traditions, it has been called the path of the Bodhisattva.

We may be mapping territories that have rarely been explored. We cannot expect others to understand it or even to understand us. We didn't even understand it until it happened. And even now we still have times when we don't understand. Somehow though, something in us knows, even feels compelled …

This is not just a knowing for ourselves. If we are willing, it is a knowing that can guide others, if they are willing. I've seen it so many times, in my own life and in the lives of others in my un-chosen role, the role not chosen with my human mind, of spiritual teacher and guide.

I've experienced the death of those I've deeply loved, including my own son. And I have come to know life continues in the invisible. I now communicate through the veils with my beloved. Most people don't believe or understand that.

I've seen it in people who have yearned for a child and experienced miscarriage. It happens in the experience of job loss and divorce or devastating financial loss. I think of my beautiful friend Emily who has cerebral palsy, which she calls CP. We dialogue together at times about the shift to another level of CP, cosmic perception.

In this second stage of our journey of co-creation, we are still in the invisible realms and dimensions not knowable from the levels of the human mind. Understanding with the rational mind is not required and may not be even available to our human selves. We need our soul knowing that can go beyond.

## Bringing Your Life into the Curriculum: Practices to See Clearly

Experience and focus on the gifts that you can see. Remembering the good times, for example, can take you through darkness. What you focus on grows.

Forgiveness is giving a gift to yourself. It releases you from the victim role. We can't be responsible for how another person chooses. Yet we can be response-able from the awareness of our souls. We can be aware that there are even stages in forgiveness. We can be gentle, patient with ourselves. Ultimately, I love what *A Course in Miracles* says: "Forgiveness is knowing there is nothing to forgive."

Seeing in the dazzling darkness can help us begin to access the gifts that we are still just recognizing. There are gifts being given that one day may ignite within us the knowing of how to guide others through. We may want to let confusion dissolve and let vision and love emerge. We can ask for that.

We can also know that sometimes the reasons are beyond our human perceptions. They may relate to expectations that were even unconscious. There may be soul assignments of which we are unaware, our own or others. Some of our soul assignments may be complete, and our human imprints keep us hanging on. From the level of soul awareness, it may be time to let go and let God.

Other soul assignments may be awaiting us or others. There may be unfinished business that our own soul needs to finish or that another soul needs to finish. The awareness of multiple realities existing simultaneously and soul assignments can dissolve judgment, if we are willing.

## The Practice of "Write Your Soul"

I invite you to take a few minutes in the silence and invite a dialogue to come. It may be between your confused self and your human self that feels it knows. There is a Self that has a higher perspective, perhaps over your whole lifetime, perhaps over multiple lifetimes.

It could be a dialogue between yourself, even your confused self, and the self of another. This has been especially useful, for me, in dealing with the death of my beloved ... when it felt that my whiteboard was erased and my heart was broken.

Sometimes our hearts are broken open for vaster soul assignments that we know not of. We have not yet experienced the realms, perhaps, where they exist. That may be our next visible or invisible platform. And it is now the in-between time. We haven't seen the visible revelations of future time.

Scribe what comes, not editing it, not judging it. Just let it reveal itself.

You can go back later, if you want to. You can even discount it later, if you want to. Yet, for these precious moments, just let your soul speak ...

# CHAPTER 13

## *Your Invisible Lineage*

BEFORE WE MOVE deeper into the garden and into the integrating of faith and trust, let's take a moment to really go into the vastness of dividing the waters above from the waters below.

What is happening is that we are transcending and including, going beyond and including all that we are awakening to in the process. In the void and darkness, before "Let there be light," there was the Spirit of God hovering over the waters.

The waters in mystical knowing symbolize the unconscious. Yet there are two dimensions, above and below. An ancient sacred knowing includes "As above, so below." What does it mean?

There is the vastness above that is pure gold, a realized state, even though we are still unconscious of it. Carl Jung called it the golden shadow. There is also the vastness below, of which we are often pretty much unaware, although at times it may sort of bite us or surprise us! This includes what we might call lessons, things our soul has come to earth to learn and perhaps to teach.

Interestingly, for me, it seems that even though some of these gifts or lessons may be hard, they can carry seeds of our soul's path of destiny. Sometimes it is as if somehow we could be advanced students in our human bodies. When that happens, we may wear interesting or difficult disguises.

We have to grow up in this lifetime, before we are ready sometimes to fully know our role of guiding others through. We come into this lifetime as an infant. Then we crawl, begin to walk, and ultimately learn at more and more complex levels. We seldom will just start out going to graduate school and understanding quantum physics. It takes time in this horizontal dimension of living.

The vastness of the waters above and the waters below will bring us potentially to the shift into our next platform. Yet it begins in the invisible. We will be imprinted and enriched by the way faith and trust work and what the mystery of our invisible lineage is giving us.

Let me share with you some of the pieces that I see, as I've discovered some of my own invisible lineage. And let me assure you that I know there is still more to come!

Boulder, Colorado, was my hometown. It was a container that held the literal fundamentalism of my birth family. And Boulder, in its potential collective vibration simultaneously, over the years of my life, expanded into a vastness that now holds such luminous structure as Naropa University, with East meeting West.

It also holds the field of integral awareness and the writing/teaching genius of Ken Wilber and people who have been his students. These writings and teachings at one point, interestingly in Walnut Creek, California, not Boulder, became guiding lights in my path. By that time, I was moving into knowing myself as a mystic, something that I never would have thought of becoming in my fundamentalist childhood.

Yet the imprints of the significance of the Bible and the teaching stories, the parables, began there in my childhood in Boulder. It happened through the simple kindergarten-type stories taught by my great-aunt Lydia. She was a Bible worker; that's what she called it at least. She mostly taught adults, yet on Sabbath mornings she taught little children, including me. I still have her Bible, written in, by her.

It was words imprinted at such a young age, *"Ask in My name and you will receive ..."* that came in that moment of deep heartbreak and yearning in my forties, leading to the voice and light experience that changed my entire life.

I was imprinted with the stories, in the setting of a Sabbath school room with a sand tray and interesting figures to move around. There were small chairs for children to sit in while my beloved aunt put the stories in really simple words. I could feel her love as she told the stories. It is so easy for a five- or six-year-old to be intrigued in the wonder. I simply felt the field of love all around.

Jesus became my friend, a loving being that little children could come to. Later, when I was a minister in Walnut Creek, I called Jesus my guru while being interviewed by a religion editor of the *Contra Costa Times*, doing a story about me. She said, "That wasn't what I wanted to hear!" A soft laugh comes as I remember.

Now, Jesus calls me friend even as I still learn and know this as part of my lineage of love, knowing Jesus as a Way Shower, as well as a Savior, when I transcend and include. I love what this has given me, in my heart, my being, in my emerging mind.

There is both darkness and light, with the light shimmering on the waters. It is on the Facebook page for Called By Love—a picture with mountains and the sea. It says "With Dr. Marj Britt and Friends." Few people know that the friends reference relates to Jesus saying, "You call me Teacher, I call you Friends."

My imprint of religion comes from lineage that goes back to the beginning of the Bible. Lineage is also in the first chapter of Matthew in the New Testament. Matthew was a Jew and went way back, recounting the begot multiple times, yearning for people of Jewish lineage to recognize their own heritage, knowing that Jesus was a Jew.

The Bible also includes stories from the three paths of Abraham— Judaism, Islam, and Christianity—that are Abraham's lineage. This is depicted as part of Site 7, Resting in the Realization, in the garden. It is on my personal Facebook page as a cover image. It's a symbol of my own lineage transcending and including.

Our lineages can be hundreds, even thousands of years old, depending on what perspective we take, depending on the window from which we choose to view it. There are so many ways that we can tell our story, or tell the parable, that we see in our life that may have parallels in others lives.

I remember a hymn that I used to play on the upright piano in the dining room when I was a child. I would sing the words … "Tell me the story of Jesus, write on my heart every word … Tell me the story most precious, sweetest that ever was heard … Tell how the angels sang, as they welcomed His birth."

What if your story is also a parable, the most precious, sweetest that ever was heard?

What if angels sang as they welcomed your birth? This is not about the story being told from the perspective of an ego lost in duality. It is the parable that can be told from the awareness of the soul.

There is hidden treasure, the Pearl of Great Price, in your story. This human and cosmic exploration seems to be part of my soul's calling, part of living your destiny, loving your life, and realizing legacy. Is it also part of yours, to find the hidden treasure in your own story?

## Practice: Bringing Your Life into the Curriculum

Find something in your life that takes you above and below, that gives you a glimpse or an insight into your potential destiny path, your soul journey.

It could start in your family of origin, your birth family. You may see the links to generations before … or even to generations to come. This will include spiritual parents or children as well as birth parents or children.

Some of it may have impacted the things you've chosen or done in your life, things like education or career, your work or what seems like a hobby.

Write your soul: "Tell me the story …"

I invite you to write about your mystery and how it may be guiding you, perhaps in simple ways, helping you, or helping others, or even the world.

Have faith and trust sometimes been shattered in earlier stages, only to be reborn as radical faith and trust in later stages? How have you grown in your knowing and awakened in your awareness?

# Code 3

## *Inspiration and Divine Imagination*

Site 3: The Jade Table
Sitting at the Drawing Board of your Mind

# CHAPTER 14

## *The Infinity of Being*

THERE IS A second archway on the path in the garden leading us toward Site 3. Charles Fillmore, the cofounder of Unity, called the third day of creation Divine Imagination. The divine part, for me, is essential. Imagination, as often understood by the human mind, isn't nearly vast enough.

This infinity of being holds the potential of downloads from beyond the rational mind, from creative imagination and source that can come in dreams, synchronicity, and other ways of mystery. It guides us in exploring the concept of reality into finding the vastness of what we do not and cannot know. It holds the energy of just Being that includes both being and doing.

My beloved friend David Jonathan asked It to speak in a dream as he prepared to co-lead with me in an intensive. It spoke in mystery: *"We live enmeshed in a life that appears to exist as defined by words and the meaning of words. And yet, if we listen, just being aware, here is Soul speaking to us. It is speaking in a language that has no words where meaning is implicit. Wading into the unconscious, we find the meaning first and how to translate the meaning into words last."* David's passion is dream work and he has done it for many years. Many of our glimpses come in dreams.

As I walk under the archway in the springtime, there are velvety green seedpods. When I reach to touch them, the softness hides their vast potential. The vine will blossom into an amazing profusion of lavender beauty. It will have the capacity of more flowering with exquisite color and an unfolding of generations to come.

If I'm walking with someone, describing this garden amidst the flames, occasionally I will be moved to give a seedpod to them and say, "You can keep it as a symbol of your infinite being." The beautiful lavender flowers are still invisible. The simple seedpod may or may not have any meaning for them.

In this journey into the unknown territories, it is all still invisible yet existing in timelessness. It's cosmic power can move the small "i" of imagination into the vastness of the All That Is, into the galaxies, as well as the smallest grain of sand. It invites, never forces. Yet I have noticed occasional two-by-fours in my life when I didn't recognize its power in the softness. Sometimes it wants my attention!

It also has its own stages of growth, developmental stages. In the winter, the vine on the arbor appears almost lifeless, brown twigs with no leaves, no vivid color. The green leaves, seedpods, and the lavender flowers are still to come. I can't make the flowering happen; it has its own timing. What I can do is nurture it, make sure it is watered and cared for, so it can grow. Without my recognition of the need for my participation, it can die.

What I've noticed, however, is that it's very impersonal in this still invisible realm. There will be seeds *I know not of* that seem to come to support the ultimate flowering of beauty. It's not that it doesn't care about me. It knows its field of Love without an opposite. It knows I am in it, in whatever stages it may appear that I'm at. This love gives us our own time, within this amazing knowing of cosmic timelessness and perfection.

It holds a usually unspoken invitation in this recognition of all-ness. It's not easy to understand. "Be ye perfect even as your Father in heaven is perfect." The words are found in Matthew 5:48. It was the way Jesus said it. Now, over two thousand years later, there are thousands of interpretations of what that means or does not mean. You will decide what it means for you.

The gift we have is that wherever we are in our seasons of growing, in our flowering, they will all be right in their own season or time, when we see through the cosmic window of this invisible timelessness.

Or, we can show up wherever we are in our time-trip of past, present, and future. Our human mind will know it as perfect or not perfect, maybe love it, hate it, or think it is horrible. We may be motivated to change it or even change others.

The field of vastness has a built-in learning system. A phrase from *A Course in Miracles* comes into my awareness … *"Choose once again …"* Such a simple gift, and sometimes it seems like we can make it so hard.

I've come to think of it as finding our center of gravity. It can shift and change, depending on which window we are looking out of into our world and depending on what season we are experiencing in our flowering. Yet it seems to be what we come back to when experiencing the changes, even surprises sometimes.

And there will come a time, at least it has for me, when our center of gravity will begin to shift into a different color of our rainbow. We will begin to see our world in a different way, even while we still may love the colors we've lived that have been part of our lives.

These shifts will come with all of the colors of the rainbow, in their own time.

It can get tougher sometimes, more like winter. Or it can get easier and better, even magical. Depending in part on our choices, we can move up or down, into the above or the below, as we deal with the unconscious within ourselves and others. We can experience it within, feel when we're aligned or not. And we experience it with others as a field between us that can light up in its different colors.

Interesting, we can usually see, yet not control, the sort of hidden things, the passages through which we travel and learn. And we know we can't control others' passages, although we may try "for their own good" or because we are "responsible."

It makes some of our roles, perhaps like parenting, interesting to navigate! A poet, Kahlil Gibran, said: "Your children are sons and daughters of Life's longing for itself. They come through you ... yet they belong not to you. You may give them your love but not your thoughts, they have their own thoughts ... Their souls dwell in the house of tomorrow, which you cannot visit, not even in your dreams."

We are maturing in our own awareness, even as we live in our outer world. Sometimes the voice of my higher self is guiding my human self with great gentleness and immense love. Sometimes there seems a sense of frustration, even urgency, like, "Will you ever learn?"

What I know is my divine self yearns for my human self to become one with it. It yearns for clear seeing in the infinity of being, the union of the opposites, about which I'm still learning. It's a strange bridge sometimes between heaven and earth, between the invisible and the visible.

I am grateful for my human, living guides. At times it is in the form of books or things I listen to. Ken Wilber has been one of my teachers. Years ago I taught Kosmic Consciousness, using a tape series where Ken Wilber is interviewed by Tami Simon, founder of Sounds True. We spent weeks in the class doing deep dives, four or five hours for each tape. Now it's available on the web as a free download.

I remember especially one profound thing. *We can see in a veiled way only one level beyond where we are* in our developmental stages, our experience of growing up that relates to our maturing in human awareness. Everything beyond that, we simply don't believe or think it's fantasy. We think it doesn't exist. And we may believe people who think that way are deluded or even crazy.

*We can see the stages, the colors that we have already lived and perhaps passed through in our growing up.* We know the texture of their colors. The imprints are in our lives; you've seen examples in my life as I've shared with you some experiences of my childhood. Each color has its own values and views of the world. We keep some, and we grow into new ones. Awareness of *transcend and include* is a huge part of seeing what is.

Wow. That helps me understand a lot … about not understanding. It gives me more patience, invites me to be kinder without making someone else wrong. Everyone is right for where they are in their way of seeing the world, when you get it from their point of view of the world. Judgment dissolves in seeing this way.

It makes me ask: How can we learn to find the bridges between these different worldviews? Is there a conveyor belt that could take us all higher, perhaps even save the world? For me, the answer to that question is love.

Sometimes I witness my mind shifting into complexity, dimensions of human crises and fear. We are in a complex time of opportunity and crises in our world and on our planet. There is no

95

arguing that point. And if I breathe into my heart, pause, what comes is the knowing that love never fails.

I don't know how it is going to work; my own life has shown up in so many complex ways. Love even has shown up in all of its own developmental stages, sort of like the God View on David Hawkins's map of consciousness. Could God View and Love View be synonyms? Maybe even words like faith and trust are like that.

And yet, knowing these things that we've shared, love, because it is love, gives me hope. It gives me a worldview with radical trust in Love as a cosmic power that can show me the way.

Love in my own life has had its own strange disguises, interesting me, attracting me, taking me deep—sometimes into territories where I felt pain or disappointment. Other times it has given me the most ecstatic gifts of joy and oneness, beyond what I could ever have even imagined.

I've learned in my seventy-five-plus years of life that there have been lots of dots to follow in my Kosmic Follow-the-Dots Coloring Book. When I follow the inner knowing, love shows me the next step, the next piece of this thousand-piece puzzle.

The picture on the cover of the puzzle box isn't available for me to see and know how it will look when it is finished. Yet somehow there is ancient memory. I find the edges, and I am aware of the colors, how they match or don't. It's up to me and other students who are learning to play this cosmic music, even though the scales may be tiring, hard, and sometimes not seem worth it!

I have a coffee cup with a beautiful picture of a Native American playing the flute, against a backdrop of a rising sun beginning to appear in a dark, star-lit sky. There are words: *"May the soothing music of Father Sky and Mother Earth forever echo in your soul."* It was my gift to my son as he was coming out of a deep crisis. In the last seven years of his life, he lived and gave the gifts of his soul.

What I hear is music emerging. My yearning and heart's intention is to be part of co-creating it. My hope is that we share this yearning. This infinity of being is complex, until it dissolves into simplicity. Don't let that throw you, scare you, or cause you to walk away.

If you aren't familiar with David Hawkins and his map of consciousness, you might want to check it out. *Letting Go* was his last book, and it is wonderful. I also love *Transcending the Levels of Consciousness*. It has a great part on the difference between love and Love.

Become an explorer, like Lewis and Clark, exploring the Louisiana Purchase. Explore your own never-mapped unknown territory. Become part of the expedition into that, for yourself and for humankind. Find a guide if you need one. Find other adventurous explorers that have heard about and want to be part of this kind of incredible journey.

## Practice: Bringing Your Life into the Curriculum

What yearnings have you felt deep within your heart and soul? Have you had glimpses of them? How do you experience their still-flowering potential? Do you pay attention to your dreams? How do you nurture the seeds, care for the glimpses of your soul, so they will grow?

Do you have a sense of where your center of gravity might be? When do you lose it and how do you find your way back? What are your practices? How do you find the stillness where you can listen to the whispers of your soul?

How do you deal with tough stuff? Where do you turn if you feel unclear? I invite you to check out www.LivingLovingLegacy.com.

Read the letter from me just below the drop-down bar. I ask some important questions:

> Are you like me? Have you yearned to find belonging, meaning and purpose all of the years of your life? Have you yearned for love in relationships, in your work, in the mundane, in all of its forms? Have you felt it, delightful, passionate, playful, juicy, tender, cosmic, in all of its expressions?
>
> Have you struggled? Are you struggling? Yearning? Have you ever felt that you didn't quite "belong" in your life? Does your heart yearn for something different than the way your life is showing up? Have you had dreams and yet find you don't know how to "go for them"?

If you want to get better acquainted with me, or with any of the people I do these dialogues with, I'd love that. All you have to do is register on the website to hear them and to get the Messages from Marj. We would love to have you be part of our live worldwide calls or listen to the replays! You can register on either website, www.LivingLovingLegacy.com or on www.CalledByLoveInstitute. com. You can learn more about how to *write your soul* as part of the process. There is also information about how to contact us with our email address: team@CalledByLove.com.

# CHAPTER 15

## *It's Written on the Wind*

IMPRINTS AND INFLUENCES happen. Downloads happen. Synchronicity happens. Out of these can come trails to be blazed.

A beautiful jade table sits under an apricot tree at Site 3 in the garden, a place where we receive glimpses of the soul, a place of divine imagination sourcing our very being. The jade table was a gift from Andy and Cathy Blanton, two beautiful beings of light. Andy was on the board of Unity of Tustin for many years and his special area of interest was the garden. I feel immense gratitude for the tender care that he gave to the garden that I love so much.

There are fig trees, apple trees, and orange trees all around. Each has its own unique seeds that hold the potential of producing after their kind.

The seeds, if nurtured, can over the years become trees themselves. Some will be become fruitful. Some will go unnoticed, perhaps even blown off by the wind. Some may find fertile ground in other places.

Let's go back, pay attention to the symbols in the third day or third code in the creation story:

"Then God said, 'Let the earth bring forth grass, the herb that yields seed, and the fruit tree that yields fruit according to its kind'" (Genesis 1:11).

Before these words in the passage of several verses, the dry land called earth and the seas appear. And there is also evening and morning. We are seeing emerging and transcending, formative stages beginning. It also includes the contrasts, the light and the dark.

If we see these invisible imprints and influences in our own lives, we can often recognize the beginning in our lives, the beginning of potentials to come. What I've noticed is that a lot of it occurs in the first two decades of our lives and then continues repeating, with new seeds being given.

We are experiencing the intersection between timelessness and time, the invisible and the visible, heaven and earth. It will happen as we move into the fourth day or the fourth stage in our garden amidst the flames. I've come to know this flame as the living flame of love.

When in the invisible, it may feel like it is still to come. Let's take a few moments in our awareness to sit at the jade table. Let's listen to the whispers of the wind.

Another scripture, for me, is profoundly related as we still sit in timelessness. Different people understand this in different ways. I'm very aware of that. Let me share the way that I have come to experience and know it in my life.

"And suddenly there came a sound from heaven, as of a rushing mighty wind, and it filled the whole house … There appeared tongues, as of fire, and they were all filled with the Holy Spirit."

This story in Acts 2:1–4 tells of the day of Pentecost. The phrase used to describe it is the "coming of the Holy Spirit," and it is about the experience of the devoted followers gathered there. They began to speak in other tongues, given to them by Spirit, and everyone heard them speak in their own language. I've gone deep, asking how these words relate profoundly to us now.

I know that *different languages for different countries* applies in very real ways to our own lives. We have different languages depending on our worldview, in different areas of our lives, like work, family, friends, or relationships of different kinds. We have a skill at translating. It is natural. We hardly notice it. What if we could learn to translate and see through the eyes of love?

The crowd's response in the story is also interesting. Some were amazed, and others were perplexed. Others mocked and said, "They are filled with new wine." It's almost stunning. It seems to me that we've all had that kind of experience at times when we try to share things that are important to us with people who may or may not understand. At least I have.

There is another piece of this story that is significant to me. It refers back to an Old Testament prophet named Joel, and the story is found in Acts 2:15–19. "I will pour out My Spirit … Your young … shall see visions. Your old … shall dream dreams. I will show wonders in heaven above. And signs in the earth beneath …"

How does all of this apply to our own lives now? When have we experienced our own whispers in the wind? Could it be, perhaps, part of the downloading of Spirit coming upon us? Have we heard, paid attention? Or have we blown it off, even mocked?

What has happened when we have seen visions or others have told us of their visions? How open have we been to dreaming dreams, even when we are older?

I am remembering in this moment a letter of recommendation that was written for me by the principal of the high school where I had been teaching when I applied for seminary. He had watched me working on my doctoral degree, dreaming my dreams. And now he was experiencing my vision that would take me out of the role in which I had worked with him at Oak Park High School in Kansas City, Missouri.

Dr. Dan Kahler wrote: "There are a lot of people who are day-dreamers. Marj is a do-dreamer." There was more to what he said, yet it is those two sentences that I remember. They are words that continue to inspire me as I continue to have visions and dream dreams, even now in my seventies. They still imprint and influence my heart and my mind and tell me that there are trails to be blazed.

How have imprints happened in your life, imprints of seeds that could produce fruit for years, even generations to come? Have you recognized that this could be a mighty rushing wind of Spirit, pouring out upon you visions for things to come?

## Practice: Bringing Your Life into the Curriculum

I invite you to take some time to go to your life review, or to glance back over the faces of love in your life. It will be a starting place. You will see the seeds that may have been part of your unconscious or conscious imprinting, seeds that may have or could have inspired you.

These seeds may have come from any of the realms of your life, your different countries where perhaps different languages were spoken. Maybe you will need to translate.

You'll also become aware of seeds potentially that weren't there for you. And in that awareness you become able to plant them yourself! It is quite amazing how this fire of the living flame of love works.

Become the architect sitting at the drawing board of your mind. Begin to more consciously receive the downloads from your higher mind, from Spirit. Let the whispers come to you, like visions and dreams. Scribe what comes, without judgment or discounting; just see what comes and put everything on the page.

Let the faces of love from your life inspire you. This may come from people you know or people you've never met! This will include faces and things, like books, not even on your radar perhaps!

Let it include education, career, purpose, and possibilities of shifts as you live the decades of your own life. I invite you to be in the border land between the invisible and the visible, between timelessness and time.

Let past, present, and future become one in the infinity of Now. See what comes if you open into prophecy and revelation, as well as visions and dreams.

I invite you to go for a hundred years even, for lineage and legacy beyond your human lifetime. I think of one hundred as the Power of One going into infinity. What are the trails to be blazed where you could apply passion, purpose, and gifts of genius that you may not yet know?

# CHAPTER 16

## *Glimpses of Your Soul*

THE SPIRIT OF God has been hovering over the waters. And now, if we are open, have done the invisible work of awareness, and if we are willing, glimpses of our soul will be accessible for us to experience.

They will still be veiled, like seeing in a mirror darkly perhaps. Yet we can feel them and somehow know when we are aligned with them. There is a resonance that we tune into; we feel it in our hearts. It is assuring and comforting. It feels safe; we know we are being guided and cared for, even when it feels demanding.

Our soul is our connection to the infinite, the essence of the All That Is. It doesn't care what we call it. That will depend on our human imprinting and knowing. We can call it Spirit, God, essence, or higher power. We can call it beloved or George or any other name. It simply is. And it loves us. It is a love without an opposite.

I experience this in what I call vertical awareness that is timeless with multiple realities existing simultaneously. These multiple realities are in the horizontal dimensions of time, as well as in the vertical. It has the dimensions of a cross. The horizontal lines can move higher or lower on the vertical dimension, sort of like an axis. Now I'm wondering, what does axis mean? I look it up, not really sure if axis is the best word to use here. Do you ever have this kind of question?

An artist once created a representation of a cross for a Palm Sunday event. It was created out of palm leaves to show how it works. People were given their own palm leaves so they could make their own moving example. I still have the paper sample made for me. I found it utterly fascinating, and even playful, like for a child. Sometimes we need simple and playful ways to learn. At least I do!

Do you ever have these kinds of wondering experiences? Like it is way too complex to understand. It's because it is, with our human minds. I don't need to read and understand a complex script before I experience the movie. And there are all kinds of movies. I don't need to know how to compose a song before I sing one.

There are romances, love stories, and songs, which I love even when they have elements of sadness or tears. I don't like movies with a lot of violence. Comedy is good. Laughter gives me a natural feeling of joy, unless it is dark; then sometimes I don't like it. We all have our preferences. They exist for me in life in similar ways. We all have our patterns. I pay attention to patterns. Do you?

Another way I experience glimpses of my soul is in the form of a triangle. At the top of my upright triangle is the word love. I feel it in my heart, always already. If I'm tuned in, it gives me passion in every area of my life. It is my code word for my true north, a compass to guide me. It goes into the highest vertical reaches.

The horizontal lines at the base are a structural necessity for pyramids to stand in their tallness, as they reach for the sky. On the left side are my gifts of genius. I know they come from Spirit and soul, as Source. Living love and consciousness with presence, thoughts, words and actions become a focus.

On the right side of this horizontal base is commitment. It is sort of a contract with my soul about doing the work, letting my soul awaken in the ongoing process within my own being. I've found important tools over the years that have helped me begin to understand things that seemed to be not understandable, some things that felt painful, hard, or difficult. It looks a bit like this ...

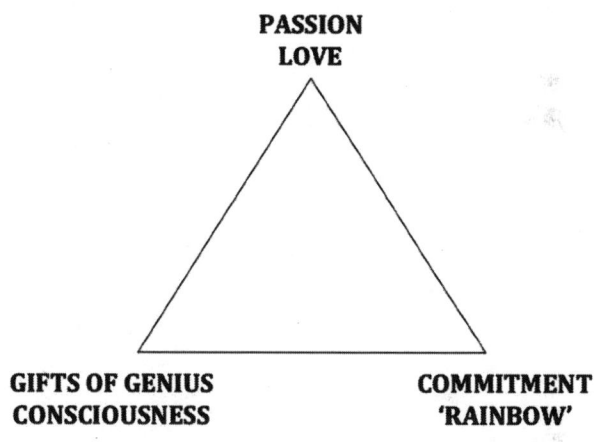

Passion Triangle

My tools have included maps of consciousness, integral and spiral dynamics, as well as the double spiral of Thomas Keating. I've found the rainbow colors in the spiral, in integral, and in the chakras useful. Russ Hudson's work with the enneagram has been very important for me.

Now, I've worked with STAGES, and we are in the process of bringing love in, with the LOVE STAGES Inventory. All of these have dimensions of developmental stages. The essential value of this began in my studies for my doctoral degree in education and still continues. And most of all, I live the stillness.

All of this can seem a bit daunting, if you think you have to study and learn it all. It could feel like you are so far behind you'll never get it or catch up. Or, it can seem exciting, if you love learning! It's different perceptions for different countries.

Then I got it! It's all experiential, and we all have experiences. And realizing that, it isn't hard to learn how it works, to begin to practice. It all can happen just seeing the rainbow, all of the colors of the rainbow, even the double rainbow that I have seen at Ragged Point. All of the colors are perfect vibrations of light.

Knowing that, pieces of complexity begin to tumble like dominos set on end. Tip the first one, just so slightly, and all of the rest go down. The learning is quite delightful, if you're into all the complexity, if you love the reading and exploration. And if you're not … well, for me, it's not required, even though it might be helpful.

The rainbow colors are living in us as vibrations of light. There are built-in systems for waking us up, helping us grow into the magnificent beings that already exist as imprints in our lives. We are growing up and waking up, always already.

The complexity dissolves into simplicity ultimately, moving toward oneness.

The entry point, for me, is love.

## Practice: Bringing Your Life into the Curriculum

Moments ago, I walked over to my desk and picked up the wedding place card that sits there. It was an experiential creative moment in the live intensive we did at Unity of Tustin in the first year of Called By Love. The intensive was on Your Gifts of Genius. It included a lot of dimensions, and the wedding place cards were one of them. We had gotten the blank place cards at a wedding store.

A card was given to each participant. "Glimpses of My Soul" was written in the lower half of the space on the front. The upper half of the card was blank, leaving room for your signature, which you could sign after you created your own triangle inside. When you finish this, you may want to create one of your own and sign it.

As I was describing my triangle for you, I was looking at the small wedding place card that I created at that moment in time. For me, it is an invitation to the sacred wedding within. It is the marriage of the essence of the All That Is, our highest self, with our human self. It may be that, for you also.

At this point it is still just a wedding invitation, with a wedding place card, and we are being invited to a cosmic wedding with the beloved. That will actually come as we do our journey together in this garden amidst the flames, as we ignite and light the Codes of Co-Creation within our own lives.

What is the one word or phrase you know you live for? What is the word that ignites your life and your soul? What is your passion? This is huge. The word *passion* is used in the week that changed the world. Sometimes it is called Holy Week; often it is called Passion Week. I will never forget my first Sunday at Unity of Tustin in 1993 on Palm Sunday. This is how significant these imprints can be.

Find one word or phrase that could describe your gifts of genius. I know that I have a gift of genius related to consciousness. And part of that for me is putting it into ordinary language for ordinary and extraordinary people. What is your one word or phrase? In the Gospel of John, creation is simply described with "In the beginning was the Word." The word is the Logos of your soul.

What are the tools of your commitment—sort of like tools of the trade? If you don't know what they are, go ahead and ask those three people who know you well, who love you and recognize who you truly are. Choose carefully whom you ask. This is not about telling you what is wrong with you. It is about finding those angels in disguise whom you already know, who really see you, and who can reflect what you may not see clearly back to you, so you can look into their mirror and know it also.

Create your own wedding place card with your own triangle, reflecting Spirit, soul, and body, your trinity being, now made visible and imprinted by you, inside.

# CHAPTER 17

## *Triangles and Pyramids*

DREAMS CONTINUE TO guide my writing. I cherish the in-between time of coming into the day. Awareness is dropping in that I've never thought of before. Fascinating. Something about a triangle standing upright in "Glimpses of Your Soul" didn't quite work for me.

I realize that seeing the triangle reaching to the sky was only the first piece. There are other triangles coming together to make up this pyramid reaching to the sky.

Early morning hours breathe in more of the mystery. First comes the awareness that there is a trinity in this—Spirit, soul, and body. Each one has a different, even predominant focus for me at different stages of my life. I know that Spirit, soul, and body, embodied human experience, are all sides of my pyramid.

Yet, in my still-fuzzy awareness, a wondering about whether there are three or four sides to a pyramid shows up. I have several sacred symbols of pyramids on the bookshelves downstairs. I've been to Egypt, seen the pyramids along the Nile. My left brain is checking in. Downstairs, I pick up my favorite crystal multicolored pyramid.

Obviously, a pyramid has four sides. What wasn't clear was the *forth* side. What does it represent?

(Weeks later, I reread my words. I know the word "forth" and "fourth" have different meanings. Looking up the word "fourth" brings more surprise. Fourth can relate to a musical interval embracing four tones of a diatonic scale. My one-time music-major mind scrambles trying to remember what diatonic means.

I go on, I find the word fourth can also mean a fourth dimension, a coordinate in addition to three rectangular coordinates, especially when interpreted as the time coordinate in a space-time continuum. There is more. The fourth dimension is something outside the range of ordinary experience.

My parallel-realities mind wonders if fourth and forth are interrelated. Forth means to go onward in time, place, and order. What are the orders of the fourth dimension and beyond?)

Awareness comes back to *forth*, and in this moment, *"Go forth and live it"* drops in. It is an invitation that I gave, standing in the back of the sanctuary at the end of every Sunday morning service for nineteen years, part of the closing that included the *Prayer of Protection* by James Dillet Freeman, Unity's poet. One of the astronauts took a copy of that prayer to the moon and left it there in a space capsule.

It feels like it's all there in its wholeness, always already, in my life. And yet there have been different phases, different developmental stages of growing up and of waking up. The growing up years of my childhood and teens are one of the faces of love, one of the faces of my pyramid. Yet I realize, of course, that I never thought about development or anything like a matrix of seven or ten-year cycles during that time! And it was happening anyway.

A subtle shift somehow seems to occur as we move toward our early adult years. There is more attraction to dreams of our future. They often include education and what may be needed for work or career. Attraction also includes the energy of love and looking for someone with whom to share love. These are pieces of another yet different face of love, where marriage, childbirth, having your own home, and jobs enter. This feels like the second of the faces of my pyramid.

The next of my faces of love has such a pure focus on Spirit, an experience that I refer to sometimes by saying, "I know I've been to the mountaintop." It includes all the years of coleading silent meditation retreats with one-hour sits several times a day. It includes the opening prayer of Sunday services with the invocation of "Come, Holy Spirit, come upon us, fill us with your Presence, fill us with your Power ..." It is the third of the faces of my pyramid, and it is still sourcing me always.

Yet, for me, the mountaintop clearly was not the end of the journey. I've always taught that this movement transcends and includes. There are changes, the good, the true, and the beautiful, the unexpected and the difficult, as we explore our unknown territory called life. We learn lessons, and we experience gifts of amazing grace. Dissolve happens, and new creation emerges, even as we go about maintaining our lives.

What I seem to be living now is somewhat different. I've called it "coming back into the marketplace with gift-bestowing hands." Sometimes I say, "I live the stillness now." As I scribe this, I realize that this is the fourth side of my pyramid, another of the faces of love. It is living with vertical awareness all of the colors of the rainbow, seeing the beauty of each of the colors in my own life and in the lives of people that have been significant in my pyramid taking form. And it is in the lives of people beyond, even in the world itself.

This brings in the next piece of knowing, a very important one. We have moved with radical trust into the third code of divine imagination. We are still in the invisible realms, still in timelessness. The descent of the Holy Spirit is still dominant. Distinctions relative to time have permeable boundaries. There are parallel realities existing simultaneously.

In the coming fourth code of divine will and understanding, the ascent of the soul will begin to take a more dominant focus in our awareness. Yet here, as we sit at the jade table in the garden amidst the flames, we access the divine architect within. We sit at the drawing board of our minds open to Spirit, waiting …

There may seem to be separation in time, relative to when things appear in awareness or form. Yet within this realm of parallel universes, we are seeing only the part of the movie that is playing through our human eyes and consciousness.

I first tapped into this knowing when I was teaching high school in the late 1970s. Somehow I got a book, copyright 1975, called *Space-Time and Beyond* written by Bob Toben, in conversation with physicists Jack Sarfatti and Fred Wolf. It had cartoon-like pictures, making it delightful and easy to read.

Page twenty-five, with its drawings, especially caught my attention: "For each of us, an indefinite number of universes exists simultaneously." We see a typical universe layer and call it real time. Yet there are unseen layers. Each universe has its own time sequence. Each universe may be a slight variation of the next one or may be entirely unrelated.

I would later hear Fred Alan Wolf speak at a Unity conference, and I would invite him to come and teach at both Unity of Walnut Creek and Unity of Tustin. He was, by then, the author of *Parallel Universes*, written in 1988. He is now well known for his many books on quantum physics and also for his participation in the movie *What the Bleep Do We Know?* Intersections in time can be quite profound ... and delightful!

## Practice: Bringing Your Life into the Curriculum

In this timelessness realm, you will simply sit with a pen in your hand, being open and ready to scribe what comes. This is not about thinking it with your intellect, not about trying to figure it out. The realm that we are accessing is beyond your human mind. It is the realm of divine mind and radical trust. There is a knowing coming out of faith in the unseen. It gives us what I often call downloads. Charles Fillmore, the cofounder of Unity, called it divine imagination.

When it drops in, it will come as glimpses, sort of like pictures or symbols perhaps. It will not include details; those will come later with the use of the rational mind that is good at filling in details. The intellect will become a servant to this higher mind.

If you are not here yet in any of these years or decades, just know it as a parallel reality, a potentiality. See what comes, knowing you will have choice.

And, be aware that the faces of love in your life may not always come in the sequence of the decades of your life. Let your soul guide you and show you when you feel the appearing and the wondering!

What are the four sides of your pyramid? Let's begin to let that knowing download glimpses in your own life. Find a place where you can sit in the stillness and simply invite these realms of awareness to bring revelation and perhaps even prophecy.

Part of you may feel like it is weird. That is because you are going outside the boundaries of what years of cultural imprints have given you. I invite you to be open to scribe what comes. Give it time. Listen for the whispers of your soul.

**The first face of love:** The growing-up years of childhood and teens perhaps, dreams of your future, maybe including school, college, or the world of work, of career. Pause for a moment and see what comes.

**The second face of love:** The years of your twenties and thirties perhaps, including stepping into education and career. It will include love and looking for someone to love, which could have even begun in the earlier years. Marriage, childbirth, home, jobs, significant events and interests will be imprinting you and potentially be part of guiding you and shaping your life. Pause for a moment and see what comes.

**The third face of love:** The years of your forties and fifties perhaps, including a feeling of being drawn to more of a focus on Spirit. An attraction to meditation, spiritual practice, and often a feeling of being called may occur. Age forty can be somewhat of a marker or a shift, it seems. Sometimes we are more able to do this as householder years may become somewhat less demanding. Pause. See what comes.

**The fourth face of love:** The years of your sixties and seventies and beyond. These years often include serving. I love to call it selfless service and giving of your gifts. It may be about guiding others with gifts of wisdom and love. It can include a knowing of how to be in the world and not of the world. There may be a dissolving of importance relative to some of the previous things that had focus in our lives. Values may seem to become more clear, with choices toward giving and simplicity. Pause. See what comes.

This is sort of like seeing the preview of a movie. Don't try to make it more than that. Just see what drops in. Scribe it, with no attachment to outcome. This is not about goal setting. This is work in the invisible realms of your soul, in timelessness. It will come more like a glimpse or flash of knowing, perhaps even like bringing something back from future time.

# CHAPTER 18

## *Your Whole Life Is Threaded with It*

I WOKE UP this morning with this title, this theme flooding into my awareness. There were some simple words that followed, seeming to be parts or paths of the mystery that came in my waking reentry into the day.

Then a sort of subtitle came, like a glimpse of how to follow the threads. *"It's woven into all the seams of the fabric of your being. And it is woven into the seams that you have sewn."*

Sewing was a part of my childhood and also my young adult years. It was an important skill often taught to young girls in the 1940s and 1950s. I know about threads and seams. As a child, I once made a whole wardrobe of doll clothes for my younger cousin, Kathy, sitting at my mother's old Singer sewing machine.

Now I could let the symbol reveal what it means in this moment of waking awareness. Two of the words that came into my mind seemed like standard stuff, applicable to most of us, *education* and *career.* The third was not standard.

It came in a phrase and was a person, identified as part of a thread: "Mrs. Plank's granddaughter." I couldn't remember her name. Interesting though, over the last several months, even for a few years, she has come into my mind. And then her first name, Louise, just dropped in.

The last name simply was gone, not there, until it was, probably fifteen minutes later. It was similar to the last name of someone else I'd known in my thirties, now nearly four decades ago. He was a person who had been somewhat pivotal in my path, like a reminder. Then, Louise's last name, Hauck, was suddenly there ...

Louise Hauck was someone I'd invited to come and teach from the platform of Unity of Tustin in the 1990s. As I often did with presenters, we went to Zov's, a wonderful Mediterranean restaurant nearby, to get something to eat ahead of time. It's a great gift to break bread together and share in the unfolding.

"Tell me about yourself," Louise said. "How did you get here, to Unity in Tustin?" In the conversation that followed, I shared a bit about my path to becoming a Unity minister and mentioned that my background was somewhat unlike my now mystical leanings. I was born in Boulder, Colorado, which included imprints of tradition and my favorite Bible verses from childhood that I knew by heart.

Louise delightfully told me, "My grandmother lived in Boulder. I used to visit her there. She lived on University, up on the hill." I told Louise I knew that area well. In fact, my piano teacher as a child had lived on University.

As Louise listened, I told her how I would go to my piano teacher's house on the bus, go up the steps of her front porch, go inside, and wait in the dining room while Mrs. Plank finished up the lesson for the piano student before me. I would sit at her dining room table where a thousand-piece puzzle was laid out for all of her students to work on while we waited for our lesson.

I can still see it all now in my awareness of past, present, and future as one. Louise's eyes became soft almost with wonder. There was a quivering kind of smile on her face as she told me, "Mrs. Plank was my grandmother ..."

Louise Hauck is now an international speaker, visionary, and intuitive. Her books include *Beyond Boundaries* and *Heart Links, Connecting with Lost Loved Ones* as well as *Streaming Consciousness: A Current of Unity*. She has had the gift of "sight" from early childhood "with the ability to move pictures forwards and backwards through time ..." I only know this now because I googled her name.

I just took these words from her website, which I'd never looked at before. Louise and I have lost touch for years. And I just clicked on Contact on her drop-down bar, all of these technology things that I'm just learning now in my seventies. I sent an e-mail, reminding her a little about who I was and said I'd love to reconnect.

I'm a bit blown away even still, now two days later, as I transcribe into a Word document my handwritten scribing of the whispers that I hear as I sit to write. It's as if in some ways Louise and I have lived some of the same kinds of experience, as if we've had what I've come to call something like parallel lives.

How often do we experience moments in time that we may or may not recognize fully? And if it comes back to us, in some strange way, how often do we say yes to exploring how the universe may be revealing part of the mystery?

## Practice: Bringing Your Life into the Curriculum

I invite you to look for a thread in your life that may be part of your own unique mystery and potentially part of a mystery greater than your personal self.

*Write your soul.* Write about the threads, the seams, the unraveling, however it may have shown up even while you still let it be mystery, or didn't.

At this moment of transcribing and recording, I've not heard back from Louise. Will I ever? Will I follow up? Who knows? Is this part of my own still-unfolding mystery? Will I recognize it? Will I know what it means?

# Timelessness
# Coming into Time

# The Visible Dimensions Action and Manifestation

"Some day, after we have mastered the wind, the waves, the tides, and gravity, we shall harness for God the energies of love. Then, for the second time in the history of the world, we will have discovered fire."

Teilhard de Chardin

# Code 4

## *Will and Understanding: The Executive Power of Mind*

Site 4: Timelessness Coming into Time

# CHAPTER 19

## *Mountaintop or Marketplace: Mountaintops of Another Kind*

THIS SEEMS TO be a time of immense acceleration of spiritual energy in the human plane. It's a waking up kind of energy, accelerating the growing-up process that has been going on in our lives and also going on with humanity for thousands of years. Both of these arenas have functioned somewhat independently, probably still will. But something very different may be emerging.

The spiritual mountaintop has always included deep spiritual knowing, sometimes including different spiritual paths, denominations, or lineages and often rigorous practices.

The marketplace has been the place for high success hopes and business model competition. It has a different mountaintop based on who wins, often translating into money and economic benchmarks.

Then there are dreamers who have a different vision, a different way of seeing. Some of the underlying values, the energy that calls, what inspires and motivates can be similar. Yet there is something that is compelling now, almost pulling from beyond.

When I look at my own life, I can clearly see the years, the stages of both the marketplace and the spiritual mountaintop. Both, for me, are important and integral parts of my journey.

My glimpses of the mountaintop in my thirties included my doctoral dissertation at the University of Massachusetts, doing research and writing on the "Life Activity Patterns of High-Success Women." I felt such curiosity, wondering how did it happen? And, of course, how did it happen for men as compared to women?

I interviewed one hundred people, fifty men and fifty women. Half of the men and women had an economic criteria involving self-made income. Half of the men and women did not have the economic criteria yet were highly successful because of other factors. An example of this was a Catholic priest who would not have qualified relative to the economic criteria yet was a significant and widely recognized leader.

It was fascinating for me. I was so curious about what the factors were and how these amazing people lived their lives. And I was aware that I would be talking with people that were immensely interesting and change makers! Many of my friends working on dissertations were finding the process grueling. I wanted to be inspired and feel the joy of it! And that is exactly what happened.

One of my goals was to apply what I learned in my own life, to teach it in seminars and workshops in the marketplace, perhaps through training in human resource development. I started my own business, Marj Britt Associates, and was being asked to speak at conferences for women in business. It was the early 1980s. A new book, *Networking: The Great New Way for Women to Get Ahead*, had just come out. I met the author, Mary-Scott Welch, loved the book, and began integrating it into my seminars and talks. Simple pieces of our story become important stepping-stones on our path.

The doctoral program at the University of Massachusetts emerged as part of my path. It was one of the world's top schools of education, pioneering a focus on experiential learning. I didn't even totally realize its status until Jean Houston asked me if I knew that, years later when she came to teach at Unity of Tustin. She was looking at my diploma on the wall of my office, and the conversation unfolded, bringing light to my lack of awareness. Clearly now, I see it was Spirit leading.

Luminaries were coming to teach us. An example was Buckminster Fuller who came as a visiting teacher, putting the doctoral students behind one-way mirrors so we could watch him working with children of different ages in the U Mass Lab School. In the evening, he would lecture to us, and the community if they desired to attend, sometimes speaking for four hours at a time. And he was in his eighties. These were inspiring and exciting times for me.

Dreams of success and impacting culture were clear motivators, including money. It was all right on track. I was in my thirties, the high-success achiever stage, the orange meme in my developmental trajectory that I now know as part of the map of consciousness, of integral or of the spiral.

There is an interview about the way I see it now with Veronika Tracy-Smith and me in dialogue. We decided to sit and talk in the garden after we had done videos on the various stages of the spiral and of the Codes of Co-Creation at Unity of Tustin. You can find it on www.CalledByLoveInstitute.com.

Now I look at those years with deep gratitude and joy of learning. And Spirit had other plans even as I was experiencing my human plans coming into amazing and successful completion.

As a child, one of my precious memories is of sitting at the feet of my grandmother as she told us stories of her life. I was there with my cousins, three boys and three girls. She told us about her life as a child and about her father, a doctor in the Kansas Territory. She became a teacher, rode sidesaddle in her long skirt to teach in her one-room schoolhouse.

And then she said, "I want all of my grandsons to become doctors." Two of them actually did. As I heard her say that, I wondered but never asked, *Why not me, Grandma?* Even though I never spoke the words, they continued to speak to me. I was the third person of her grandchildren to become a doctor, a doctor of education, combining both her life and her father's. I knew I would be a role model for other women. It is still why I continue to use Dr. as part of my name.

An experience of gratitude was very much a part of my life. I realized how far I had come, especially as I became aware of the cultural imprints experienced by women. I felt a deep commitment to be part of the change that I yearned for myself. Yet it wasn't just about women. I was the mother of a son, and I wanted a different world for him also. It was all part of my heart's yearning.

## Practice: Bringing Your Life into the Curriculum

What calls you? How do you respond? Do you recognize stages of both the marketplace and the mountaintop in your life? Do you see your high-success achiever stage also known as the orange meme?

If you are wondering about what the orange meme is, it is part of the framework of integral and spiral dynamics. Now it is beginning to be integrated into the language of our culture. And it is a fabulous example of different languages for different countries and the importance of learning to translate.

Other stages will be there also. Do you recognize them? Can you describe them, as if from a witness state?

What imprints did you experience from your family, tribe, culture? How did they unconsciously or consciously influence your life? Who have been the way showers in your journey, significant influencers in different stages of your life?

I invite you to use your own life as research in the process. Explore as someone who can be part of understanding, or even teaching consciousness. Take the deep dive with levels of curiosity, as if you are witnessing it.

Breathe deeply, go into that alignment with the All That Is, and scribe what comes.

## Mountaintops of Another Kind

Falling in love is a profound igniter of shifts in our lives. I graduated from U Mass with the doctoral degree. And instead of flying to the East Coast to attend my own doctoral graduation, I chose to be in Kansas City at Unity Village attending my second husband's graduation from seminary!

Love had simply dissolved one value structure and put in place another one. I had not planned it or even tried to make it happen. My beloved friend Robert Hudson, whom I knew from the Kansas City Ski Club, had invited me to hear Jean Houston speak at a conference at Unity Village. He happened to introduce me to his seminary classmate, who became my husband within six months.

I smile when I realize now how quickly things can change in this path of love! Even the marriage, within two years, was in a process of dissolve, and I was in a process that I now describe as being called by God. It would lead me to seminary, and my life would change. I became a Unity minister. Without John in my life and my marriage to him that didn't last, it might not have happened. We can see mysterious, connecting links in our lives if we look with the eyes of the soul and see through the lens of love.

The path of love brought me to a different mountain, yet the mountaintop yearning was still there. It would include studying and even researching high success in ministry and in churches, all part of the call of God that I was now experiencing. Spirit uses all of our gifts of genius in the greater plans that will emerge as we are called. And we may experience that we are called in different forms at different stages in our lives.

Part of Spirit using my gifts included twenty-five years as a senior minister in three churches, what I now call the bricks and mortar platform stage of my life. It would include coleading silent meditation retreats for many years in California, Colorado, and at Unity Village with my beloved Paul, whom I met when I was in seminary. The gift of our beautiful spiritual partnership was part of taking me to the spiritual mountaintop through hour-long sits in the silence several times a day in those silent retreats.

Over two decades, the mind that wrote the dissertation on success would dissolve in the stillness. The pinnacle of the mountaintop had been reached. And yet, Spirit and love still had other plans. Being called by love was the next emergence. It would include coming back down the mountain, coming back into the marketplace with gift-bestowing hands. Again, I didn't plan it, and it happened anyway.

The paths of being called by God and being called by love have both held deep passion, total devotion, and following the points of light. There has been immense delight and joy, beauty, gratitude, and love. And both have included elements of surprise, even shock, and change.

I don't know if it is that way for everyone. It has been for me. In my seventies now, I have experienced the highest levels of ecstatic bliss and love beyond what I could have ever humanly imagined.

And I've experienced deep levels of sorrow and grief, where my human self had no clue about how to navigate it. I called it tsunamis, earthquakes, and womb houses. It became part of the energy that launched the original website for Called By Love.

Now, nearly four years from the time of writing what became the first blog post for Called By Love, I am seeing clearly. My life is being directed by a power greater than my human mind or self. I call it the Beloved. I also know it as my soul.

I am living the stillness of the mountaintop in the world and the mystery of what it means to be called by love is revealing itself every day. I know the deep meaning of the principle that *A Course in Miracles* teaches: *Miracles are natural. When they are not happening, something has gone wrong.*

What can go wrong is that we can forget to listen, forget to pay attention, forget to follow the whispers that we hear. We can move out of alignment, and then we feel the strange bumps of missing the direction. It requires us to listen, to remember love, and to "choose once again."

So the question about mountaintop or marketplace, for me, becomes both/and. Things that are part of an old paradigm will dissolve; they have completed their purpose, even though they were very significant and totally essential in our soul's unfolding journey.

A new beginning is emerging. A new paradigm is becoming accessible. It can be part of the realms that Thomas Hübl speaks of when he talks of "future time that genius people can know and reach." It's interesting. I've taught gifts of genius for years, and I had never made that connection. Of course ... we keep learning with each other.

It comes in golden thread connections that reveal themselves in glimpses and with surprise at times. Love is the field, the container, and the recognizable motive. Yet it is a pure love in the highest reaches of mountaintop altitudes.

Intersections in time can change our lives if we recognize them. I yearn for you to know how important this is. Let me remind you again. You can click on any of the pictures of the people on our telesummit website. After their bios, I write about the intersection in time that I experienced with each of them. At the bottom of the homepage, you will find a section called Co-Creators, where all of their websites are available for you to find. Intersections in time can be part of your destiny path.

The call that I experienced to do www.LivingLovingLegacy.com was totally clear and totally daunting, simultaneously. I didn't know how to do telesummits! When we are called, it will often take us into territories that we never would have humanly imagined.

You will recognize your own call in your heart. Listen; it is singing the song of your soul. It is the beloved, visible and invisible, both/and, calling you. Maybe, if you are like me, it will be so simple that you will describe it in one word. For me, that word is love.

## Practice: Bringing Your Life into the Curriculum

How have you experienced changes in what calls you? How has it been surprising or daunting? How have you responded?

Has falling in love been a profound igniter of shifts? Can you see the impact?

Who were important intersections in time for you? How did some of these golden thread crossings lead you, guide you, open you, or even close you?

How have miracles been natural in your life? What happens when things go wrong? How do you work with it when things don't go the way you thought they would, not as you planned? Do you find a different way?

Is there one word or a phrase that you know to be calling you, that is singing the song of your soul?

Choose one or more of these to explore. Take the deep dive with it. Scribe what comes.

# CHAPTER 20

## *Surprise! Life Happens, and Time Goes into Shift!*

IN JUST A few years, we've come a long way on our invisible platform! A new website for Called By Love Institute has birthed with a soft launch. I thought I had the schedule planned clear through the end of the year for my blog posts. I had even sent it to our wonderful team; they had put it up on the calendar. It looked like it was written in stone.

Have you ever had this experience in your life? Surprise! Shift happens.

Sometimes it happens because of good things like you get a promotion and have to move, or you finish something and go on to the next thing that you are eagerly anticipating.

Sometimes it is because of something that is really hard, like illness, or divorce, an accident, or even the death of someone you deeply loved. You sometimes feel like you go into a void, a blank spot. Everything gets sort of blurry.

This is part of the spiral, part of the many colors, part of the cycles of time, part of what I simply call living on the human plane. Change happens.

We've got a good shift happening! I'm in a very accelerated learning process. I am going through the shifts from a brick-and-mortar platform to my new world of the invisible platform of the worldwide web. I am loving it, and I am also still learning things every single day!

All of the learning is really good for me—even when I'm searching, even if I am in my seventies with a whole lot of amazing life experience and some credentials. It is all experiential learning! Our learning and where it leads us together never stops. It keeps spiraling higher and deeper.

So here is what's happening. Right now, in this moment of time, we are in an extremely important launch of *Your Life as a Sacred Love Story*. It needs to be at the forefront of our gaze, where we put all of our attention. What could be more important than that?

Who you are, what your love story is, and realizing how your love story is sacred—that is one of the most important things that you could ever get in your life.

It could change everything, how you understand "Why?" even. It could give you the key to your genius and how your future self is yearning to give it to you now. This is too important. I don't want to split attention in any way that would divert you from getting it.

So, change happens. Our schedule of dates will change to reflect the priority. I will share in my blog posts the amazing process of creation happening right now, in my life, your life, and in our co-creating together. A gentle smile of recognition comes as I realize, "This vibration is working me …"

Welcome aboard this rapidly moving shift into the vastness! I'm trying to think of the symbol that could represent how it feels. Is it like Japan's high-speed bullet train? Or could it even be like a rocket launch for a communication satellite, or even a moon launch of a space capsule going on a trajectory toward the moon, with many in-course corrections from Houston? Will it be a shooting star or a nova, a star showing a large increase in brightness'?

This is the way that the spiral works! We are taken higher and deeper. We go into vastness we couldn't have even imagined, even months, certainly years ago. Our minds weren't wired for it yet.

As we go higher, the light shines on things that are deeper in our unconscious, parts of our shadow, learning from the realms of duality, including loss. It is a double spiral. Each shift to a higher realm of the spiral shines the light on a deeper hidden realm, perhaps of pain, perhaps of potential.

This amazing process of grace also includes our golden shadow, our real self, the genius that our soul yearns to give us from what we see as future time, what our soul knows as timelessness.

What will be so important is our continuing communication. How do we do it on this new-for-us, at least new-for-me, invisible platform of the worldwide web? We will be doing it with comments, questions, and even the dislikes that so many of us dislike. It will all be information leading to co-creation. It will be happening on the worldwide calls, with people sharing how it is working for them, with lots of space for asking questions and learning.

We will be like a collective nova, a star with a large increase in brightness. We will let that brightness shine in all of our relationships. We will do it when we invite our friends or when we share with friends.

This is actually a very sacred part of our life as a sacred love story. You may have noticed the your or my changes to our and we. It reflects awareness that we have entered what some have called the we-space. It is leading us into the oneness that transcends yet includes our unique selves. This is a very holy journey that we are on.

Part of this is a very profound process that includes shifts-within-shifts movement that is horizontal as well as vertical! We experience the new. We receive it and begin to integrate it. Then we often shift into active energy, sharing what we have learned, what we are passionate about.

And we are launching!

## Practice: Bringing Your Life into the Curriculum

I invite you to sit in the stillness again as you open to witnessing your own bullet train of change happening. Take a few moments to simply breathe and open into the realms of higher awareness.

When have you had a schedule planned, one sort of written in stone? How did the surprise happen? How did life change? What have been the good things, as well as the hard things, that have come out of it? Did it bring an accelerated learning process into your life? How has your learning experience spiraled, higher and deeper?

Consider how this could be opening into a shift, into a higher realm that requires shining the light on a deeper, hidden realm. It may be one of pain, initially at least, which moves into potential that you could not have humanly imagined.

How have you given your attention to change? Has it been in the forefront of your gaze? What is most important about this for you? Have you been able to shift in order to reflect the priority?

Have there been shifts from more of an individual space to more of a we-space? Can you see this happening more than once, at different times in your life?

Were there times when you were in a receiving energy? Have new things come in and, after a time perhaps, been integrated into what feels like you? Did you shift into active energy, even sharing what you became passionate about?

After sitting with some of these questions, just breathe again. And begin to scribe what comes. How are you launching?

Have you been willing to embrace surprise and change? Has it sometimes taken time?

# CHAPTER 21

## *Oh ... We're There Already*

AFTER MY FATHER died when I was eleven years old, my mother had a really hard time finding her way. She bought a small travel trailer, 1950s style, hitched it to the back of our Buick, and we set out ... toward an unknown destination.

My younger brother and I were the map readers and her companions in this adventure to help her find her way out of the void. We read Burma Shave signs along the highways as we played alphabet games, often asking, "Are we there yet?"

And now here we are, you and I, in our adventure of exploring the maps and stages of creation. We've traveled through darkness and light. We opened into faith and radical trust. We've explored our gifts of genius and glimpses of our souls.

I was in the midst of my deep commitment to daily writing and emerging curriculum shifted my focus into the soft launch of www.CalledByLoveInstitute.com. It asked me to write blogs and content. Life has its content even when we set our intentions.

My wondering mind kept asking, *How will I bring this shift into the fourth stage of this creation story?* Something in me kept saying, "This time it is from the soul. It has to be different."

My human mind knows that there is more. Yet it also knows that this time, this turn of the spiral, it will be going higher and deeper. This time, higher mind, the essence of the soul, will be leading and guiding. Through so many years of my life, I've followed the ways of goals. Later that shifted to intentions.

It's been actually quite wonderful, magnificent at times, with manifestation and what the world would call success. Yet somehow, I've always known there is more. And sometimes I don't see it yet, even when so many clues and glimpses have affirmed this knowing that comes from beyond my human mind.

It seems to descend, to drop into my heart. It fills me almost with an ecstatic grace. It comes and envelops my being. It is soft and tender, even while it is calling me. When it comes, it is easy to miss if I'm not paying attention.

It is somewhat like a dream. When I wake up in the morning, if I don't write it down, chances are that it will be gone. I won't remember it. I've begun to realize that even though it seems elusive, it is actually me that goes away.

So this morning, after three months of writing distractions, I am sitting here writing. It is flowing like a mighty river, giving itself to me, penetrating and imprinting my very being. That is when I realized it has already happened!

We are already in the next stage. The visible is here already in my writing for the prelaunch on www.CalledByLoveInstitute.com. It is everywhere, in all of the pieces that I'm writing for *Your Life as a Sacred Love Story*. It has even given itself more dimensions than I had planned, like three-minute videos, which I thought that I would never do. Surprise!

Now that I realized that we are already there, I can see what I've known all along the way. "I Am That, Always Already" is real, even when it is not yet manifest or clear to my human mind.

It's like it sort of pops. Suddenly I can see more clearly. And then I see how it has been giving itself, guiding me, all along. More pieces of the puzzle begin showing up—people, ideas, resources, and structures of manifestation. It often has an element of synchronicity.

There is a synergy present that is about "When two or three are gathered ..." It comes in the gathering in that consciousness. If you are wondering, yes, this is that forever reoccurring scriptural download thing that comes from my childhood imprinting. The scripture is found in Matthew 18:20.

It has its own timing. *The cause is from beyond time and is waiting for the field in the world, including me, to be ripe for it to give birth.* It is easier to see sometimes when you look back. You can identify how so many pieces, events, people, and moments in time came, all of it working together to give birth to what is coming.

Called By Love Institute is an example. It began as what I might call a divine idea dropping in over four years ago. Codes of Co-Creation is another example. It began when I was in seminary in 1985! In both and in all of the events of my life, there have been many dance steps for me to learn, to live, to be, and to do in the realms of time.

What appears as duality, the "no" of the human plane, directed and redirected me as often as the "yes"! We are going into countries we've never been in before, individually and collectively, at least consciously. They are new paradigms of the soul. Somehow we have been called to be explorers.

We will lay new cosmic grooves. We will become way showers and guides for ourselves and for others. And first, we have to go into an unknown territory, explore it, and map it.

We have to do it with our feet on the ground, even as our essence, our heart, and our higher mind are aligned with and being directed from what is beyond our human mind. Some would call it Source. Some would call it God. I call it Beloved.

How did it happen that we are here together? There used to be a radio show in the early days of radio. I remember the voice still. However, now I've changed it a bit. It would say: "Who knows what lurks in the hearts of man?" There was a pause followed by "Only the shadow knows …" with a sinister laugh, although I probably didn't know that word then.

Now I hear a gentle, even playful laugh. The radio show of my childhood has a re-interpretation. The sinister lurking is gone, and the question becomes, "Who knows what is in our hearts?" It is a golden shadow that reveals itself now as loving, inviting, and pure.

We are being called together into a potential that we can hardly imagine. It is full, magnificent, and good. It is not just for ourselves; it is also for people we love. It is for each other, and it is for the world.

## Practice: Bringing Your Life into the Curriculum

Take some time to just sit in the silence. Just commit to being in the stillness where the beloved, your soul, can simply drop in … I promise you, it is yearning to be with you.

Ask: "What am I being called to explore beyond what my human mind knows, for myself, for others, and for the world?"

154

A scriptural energy supports us, if we are open to it: "Ask and you will receive …" Matthew 7:7 is where you will find it.

Scribe. If you are willing, see what comes …

Don't try to figure it out with your human mind; just listen to the whispers of your soul. And don't even attempt to do the how, even though it may give you some clues or glimpses from time to time. This is not for your human mind, no matter how brilliant it is, to figure out.

Transcribe. After I'm finished, as I am doing now, I transcribe it into Word.

And for those who may have some of the same imprints that I do, or are interested in exploring them, I love being aware that "In the Beginning was the Word …"

It is the creation story in one verse! It is found in John 1:1 and is absolutely written on my heart!

# CHAPTER 22

## *The Platform of You*

ON A TUESDAY morning early in the 2016 primary season, I was aware that the first debate of the Democratic candidates for the United States presidential campaign was going to be live on CNN. Part of my heart connected with past moments in time.

I spoke to John Robinson, one of our core team from the very beginning of Called By Love. "I may put on my old George McGovern delegate badge and turn on my non-digital television and hope that I can get it. Although, I'm not sure. Cox cable is switching over to all digital! God, it is hard for me to adapt to all of these postmodern changes in parts of my life." We laughed.

Well, I got it on my computer, not on cable, so there will be a shopping trip for a new television potentially. Our lives are filled with past, present, and future, all a part of our now, always already experience. Our minds and our hearts, even our physical lives move into "An update is available. Click here to install."

How many platforms have you had in your life? The Democratic and Republican Conventions will have platform committees to work on rewriting their platforms. Have I told you I have a BA and an MA in political science? Are you surprised?

What surprises have you not talked about that seem to be just part of your past?

I promised in our third prelaunch e-mail, "Why is it Unique and Different?" that I would answer the question about why I might be a guide for you in knowing your life as a sacred love story. And I said as I described my knowing of why, I would guide you in being able to describe "your why."

"It's a hybrid kind of thing. I think you may recognize yourself... in me." One of the reasons that I am an amazing guide for this kind of journey is that I know my own hybrid kind of life. You also have that hybrid kind of life. It is part of what makes you extraordinary. It is also the I Am source of your own gifts of genius. And do you know your I Am and my I Am are one?

I'm going to use an unusual template to share "why I am a potential guide" and then use that as a map to guide you in describing your own why. I've had a stranger in a strange land relationship with politics, where my major spanned international diplomacy, constitutional law, and public administration.

The template model to which I was guided by my curiosity, as well as the need for a memory update, comes from George McGovern, via Google and Wikipedia. It's incredible what is available in today's world of technology!

Here is the template for you to apply to your own life. I'll use my own life as an example so you can get the idea of how it works.

**Early years and early education:**
For me, this involves my childhood in Boulder, Colorado, my imprint from my family, the fundamentalist church and private church

schools that gave me the love of the Bible. Then it was literal; now it is mystical knowing.

**Love, marriage, and the birth of a child:**
Finding myself in love's emergence ... beyond my tribe. Co-creating a home, seeking a path that would give us jobs and maybe have career potential, as well as creating substance for our lives, giving meaning and purpose.

**Later education and early career:**
Returning to school, knowing I wanted to be able to provide, if necessary, a college education for my son. William Jewell College, a major in political science, with education as a back-up plan. Two decades of teaching in public education: seventh and eighth grade, social studies and English; eleventh and twelfth grade, sociology and psychology. Co-creating an alternative school for high school students who had a tough time in regular school settings. Master's degree, University of Colorado, pre-law intention with a scholarship and then a decision not to go. *(Does any wondering come up for you when you read some of this? I hope so. It will make it easier to find your own whys in your own soul's journey.)*

**Shifts, changes, the further reaches:**
Divorce and the in-between years ... love and yearning, knowing there had to be more. Publishing, Feminist Press, Long Island, New York. Doctoral degree, University of Massachusetts, curriculum, counseling, psychological education. Dissertation on life patterns of high success *(Breathe ...).*

**Called by God:**
A voice and light experience, my call to ministry. Unity minister for three decades: senior minister, Unity of Walnut Creek and Unity of Tustin, co-creating a Campus of Consciousness. Unity national leadership, church growth and development, as well as Unity seminary

board. Passionate, even voracious exploration of consciousness and the many paths to God. Co-leading five-day silent meditation retreats.

**Called By Love:**
**Downloads and inner knowing amidst outer change**
Monthly live intensives on Codes of Co-Creation, shift from a visible platform to invisible platform of the web. Master teachers who changed my life. Telesummit, www.LivingLovingLegacy.com. Deep-dive telecourses. Shift to nonprofit mind-set, www.CalledByLoveInstitute. com, with 501(c)3 status, worldwide calls, voice blog.

**The later years, legacy and beyond:**
After realization, there is more. It has been called coming back into the marketplace with gift-bestowing hands. Jesus called it "You are the Light of the World." It comes through you and as you. You live it in the world. This stage is, for me, in emergence. Glimpses include this book, with awareness of "A Garden amidst the Flames" as part of my living flame of love.

## Practice: Bringing Your Life into the Curriculum

Now, reverse order these. Then you will know where the gold is. This is the way that transcend and include works. Seventy-five years of my life and there are stories to tell with every line. It will be the same with your life regardless of your age.

This is the journey of your soul, seen through the eyes of the soul. You'll notice that there are things that would not be part of any resume. And there are missing pieces that are still left unspoken, perhaps to be spoken at another time.

Looking back, often we can see souls who have been significant over many stages in our lives. Ed Casey, my beloved friend of more than 40 years says, "We were important cogs in each other's wheel of life." When Ed talked about going back to college when we were both in our 30's, I was the one who said "Do it!" And, he was that cog of support for me when I followed my emerging dream, going to New York, the beginning of my path toward my doctoral degree.

These are heart connections to be treasured. In our 70's, I will never forget the long distance call when I was feeling so lost in grief. Ed's words, "We will make it through this ..." felt like a lifeline as I was struggling to even breathe. Several years later we went to his nephew's pre-wedding celebration with a 1970's theme. We wore George McGovern delegate badges!

Who have been the souls that are interconnecting cogs in your wheel of life? How have you reached out to them? Have you been that for others?

Most of all, this is simply part of the exploring of consciousness, the journey that we will move toward potentially, into the unknowing and beyond. Another question: Can you see clearly where the monumental leap is?

It may be important for you to have a guide that you can trust. Only you will determine that. Our lives will be different. We will learn from each other and all adventurous souls on this sacred exploration.

If you google George McGovern on Wikipedia, you will see he has ten categories that expand into an amazing description of a life fully lived. It includes flying thirty-five missions over German-occupied Europe with a hazardous emergency landing of his damaged plane and saving his crew. There is losing to Richard Nixon in one of the biggest landslides in American electoral history. It also includes being defeated in a bid for a fourth term in the U.S. Senate.

There will potentially be some hazardous emergency landings in your life, as well as losses and defeats. Looking back, you may recognize that visionaries are often ahead of their time, and they are not necessarily supported by popular vote. Yet there is something beyond that. You may be one of those genius people coming back from future time.

Find your seven to ten categories. You will choose your own. Mine are different than George McGovern's, and yours will be also. With times of stillness supporting you, scribe what comes. You don't have to share it with anyone. However, you might want to, as you begin to see how the universe brings together co-creators for cosmic missions that may, just perhaps, be part of changing the world.

Love is a conveyor belt. We are called by love in all of the areas of our lives in which we have felt passion, yearning, or longing. We learn about what that means together. What I know: Some of what you write for your seven to ten categories will be what the universe, Spirit, essence, God, or whatever you call it will use. It will happen through you, and as you, and will be part of changing the world, if you are willing. And all it takes is a little willingness!

# CHAPTER 23

## Creating, Manifesting, and Rediscovering Passion

IN THE LAST year of my seminary training, one of the benchmarks was giving our chapel talk. It was about bringing together everything we had learned in a new, creative, passionate form.

Having completed the defense of dissertation at U Mass, I saw some equivalency in this sacred continuation of emergence. Looking back, now nearly three decades later, I see patterns of birthing, growing, maintaining, dissolving, and discovering occurring and reoccurring multiple times in my life.

The title of my chapel talk was "The Work of Your Life." I realize now that it is still in progress! The way it is showing up at a very deep level in this moment is profoundly about rediscovering passion.

It feels playful and also adventurous. It is filled with delight and at times surprise. There is recognition of both the difficult and the joyful. It is as if it all exists in a field of simple peace, even as it scintillates with the aliveness of passion.

The work of my life is no longer defined by roles, although there have been many roles. Most of them I've loved, and there have been a few that didn't seem to be a match. Interestingly though, some of these have even reappeared in new context as a part of a whole at later times in my life!

I've begun to see a kind of scaffolding, a way that everything builds upon what has come before, transcending yet including while becoming more. There is a spiraling, higher and deeper, that includes stages and cycles in time.

Part of my own rediscovering passion is continuing to learn, to open into the unknowing, the vastness beyond that which has come before. A playful and powerful way to do this is in the kind of field trip experience that I sometimes assign for bringing your life into the curriculum.

Have you ever deeply considered what the word *field* could mean? For me, what it now offers is a field of consciousness, a platform that holds mostly an invisible vibration. What comes to mind is the Rumi poem that I quote so much: *"There is a field beyond right and wrong ... I will meet you there."* For me, that field is love without an opposite. It is where I want to live now.

And there are other fields in our growing up and waking-up process. Each has its own patterns and viewpoints, values, positions, and purposes. Every single one of them in my own life has been essential, profoundly significant, and important. There have been different manifestations to experience. New skills and abilities also come online in each field. It is like a house or building with different floors and differently decorated rooms on each floor.

Which takes me back to my chapel talk in seminary. The night before I gave the talk, I had a dream about moving into a new penthouse suite on the top floor of a beautiful apartment building.

Looking at the view was so amazing. Then there was a knock on the door. It was the custodian saying there was a lot of stuff in my storage room in the basement that needed to be cleaned up and I needed to take care of that. I included the dream in my chapel talk the next day!

I loved doing a field trip over the last week to participate in a five-day intensive on the STAGES Inventory developed by Terri O'Fallon. The intensive was taught by Terri O'Fallon and Kim Barta. Kim is Terri's younger brother, yet they didn't discover their shared passions, which would lead to the synergy of their work, until only a few years ago, even though they are part of the same family! The intensive was extremely powerful and exquisite in its design. It was filled with experiential as well as cognitive learning.

A beautiful takeaway was about shadow crashes related to a driver being damaged in an earlier stage. I'd never heard the phrase shadow crashes until I heard Kim speak of it and then talk about the powerful process of recovering into the full potentials of stages beyond.

I loved it when Kim said, as I was later telling him about my dream, "It's interesting that someone in the penthouse doesn't have access always to the entire building. And isn't it fascinating that the custodian does."

What an amazing team they make with Terri's work so deeply immersed in research, education, and her related life experiences while Kim is deeply immersed in years of being a therapist. The synergy of their work together is incredible.

Another significant insight for me was when Awareness replaced thoughts as a primary modality. Over and over again, I experienced a feeling of such immense gratitude. Finally I was hearing descriptions that felt like my own life was included. The feeling that I've had so many times of being a stranger in a strange land had found a setting in which it could dissolve.

Intuitively, I know that love is a field in which this happens. I've yearned to know more about how love moves as a conveyor belt in our lives. And I am delighted that Terri O'Fallon and I have now co-created a LOVE STAGES Inventory available on www.CalledByLoveInstitute.com, which will work with the STAGES platform. I am seeing how all of the stages of my life, the platforms of my own life, have been part of bringing me to this moment of collaboration.

This morning, upon returning, I listened to a video done by one of my coaches, Jeff Walker, from whom I am learning about what is, for me, the strange world of the Internet platform. He was talking about how it all starts in our mind and that we create there before we create out in the world. I would add, it starts in my heart.

Then the stunning moment came. He said, "We grow it from the ether, and that is absolutely awesome. And you have to keep on stepping up, growing your vision." Part of it is hanging out with people and around people who support you and that support you having a bigger vision.

What was really stunning for me was Jeff's use of the word "ether." Charles Fillmore, the cofounder of Unity, used that word. It's not one that I hear a lot now. It was very powerful for me to hear Jeff connect it with creation. It was sort of a symbol, like an affirmation of a connection in consciousness.

Rediscovering passion is as often invisible as visible. The invisible, where I find the changeless, is as real as the visible. The presence of love is there, vibrant, strong, courageous, and alive. It is also tender, sweet, cherishing, and even playful. Somehow purpose, passion, and the work of my life intermingle. They explore and co-create together, all as faces of love.

## Practice: Bringing Your Life into the Curriculum

Take some time to go into the stillness and let it reveal Itself. Look for patterns repeating higher and deeper, repeating with different levels of awareness in different stages of your life. Jot down a few notes about them. If you don't record them, there is a large possibility that you will forget.

Think about people who have come into your life at different moments in time, guided you, or been part of the patterns or the stages in your life. Others may have helped you, perhaps, in understanding or interpreting them.

It could be someone like Terri O'Fallon who spent years exploring, not only as a researcher but also as a teacher, as well as being in administrative settings. Or it could be someone like Kim Barta who does the on-the-ground work in therapy, working with clients to help them move through the problems, experiences, or yearnings in their own lives.

Go into the silence. Invite faces of love who have been part of your sacred love story, souls who have been part of your thousand-piece puzzle, to come into awareness.

See if you can find those people, places, and parallels in your life. See if you can recognize your experiences of creating, birthing, manifesting, maintaining, and at times seeing the dissolve. And then, ultimately, see if you can find experiencing the rediscovery of a new kind of passion.

It is all there for you, to see it and to be it. I invite you to sit in the stillness. Listen to your heart. Scribe what comes ...

# CHAPTER 24

## *Repeating Colors of Your Rainbow Manifestation*

## *Glimpses of Double Rainbows and Beyond*

SOMETIMES THINGS COME, and it just seems like we are repeating ourselves. We can often recognize it in others, not always in ourselves. When we recognize it, we may feel impatience with ourselves or others, with differing degrees of understanding.

Is there a different way to look at it? Could it be like a life review, especially if it comes in a theta state kind of awareness, associated with dreams and revelations, when you are coming out of sleep, a kind of entering the morning gently experience, offering you a higher knowing?

Could it be a way of seeing how all of the puzzle pieces fit and link together, even though they show up in different times and colors of the rainbow? Are answers being given that are revelations, not just forgetfulness, old-age, or otherwise?

Destiny paths, for me, can be seen, even mapped, when we unveil our soul's invisible codes from levels of awareness that are beyond the thinking mind. As we experience the fourth stage of co-creation and beyond, in our garden of being and becoming, a different kind of awareness comes to the forefront. It is an awareness of the manifest realm and our place in it.

It's not just impersonal. It is possible for me to be part of shaping this! And there are others around who are encouraging, or not, and influencing that awareness. There are repeating patterns, inviting deeper work with forgiveness and greater levels of understanding. It will bring healing at higher octaves, for self and others.

There are reiterating patterns of energy fields also coming back for higher-octave manifestation, non-dual awareness that invites the laying of new cosmic grooves, where manifestation may appear differently, perhaps for new generations.

This is conveyor belt awareness of seeing with new eyes when a new time for manifestation has ripened. There may be unfinished business, where iron curtains may be dissolving, preparing the way for new awareness to come.

I've pondered and questioned how to write about these things. The complexities of formlessness moving into form, of timelessness coming into time, can be very different, complex, and viewed through many different lenses.

Would it be of value to go back and relook at my own story, see if there are themes that I can see repeating, even in monumental leaps into perhaps second and even third tiers of consciousness? Could it all be like an ice-cream store, where there are many flavors, even different stores, like Baskin Robbins with thirty-one flavors? Or like many different kinds of tea, including some with caffeine and some non-caffeinated?

Is it about different platforms, even different tiers representing huge shifts in consciousness? Is there even an ending or a beginning? So maybe we can just jump in. I'll go first, and if you will follow me, maybe we can share our stories, our experiences, and learn from them.

When does your life as a sacred love story actually begin? Is it at birth, or is it in the womb or even before? If you happen to be someone like me, you may also hold a weird belief that is seldom spoken of ... that we choose our parents, from the level of the soul before we come into this plane.

Seeing through this lens, I perceive Boulder, Colorado, where my parents lived, as one of the things that my soul considered. It becomes part of my journey of manifestation with magical imprints of beauty, the mountains and flatirons, even the Boulder environment that was part of the first twenty years of my life.

The decades of my own life have shown up with very different stories and ways of manifestation in my unfolding world. In all of the years of teaching and ministry with people, so many have shared stories that are unlike my own in so many different ways. In my weird way, I see it all as perfect, pieces of why we came.

It feels to me now that this is related to our individual soul's destiny, the gifts we've come to give as well as the lessons we've come to learn. There is clear awareness in my own life that unfinished business can bring souls back together!

Rather than feeling that I am just repeating myself, see if you can identify, in order to explore, higher octaves and repeating patterns with opportunities to learn and grow. Ultimately, for me, this takes us all the way to awareness of soul groups, even one soul and beyond.

The first decade of my life unfolded in what I experienced as a world filled with love, safety, and security. I felt it, even though it was the 1940s and a war was going on in the world beyond my awareness.

A wound to my knowing of blind faith occurred when I was eleven years old and my father died very unexpectedly. Now I call it a holy wound. I was Daddy's girl; he knew it, I knew it, and everyone knew it. And now, how could I live without his arms to hold me and make my life safe and happy?

Yet it opened me into another world. My mother ran away from her grief, taking my little brother and me with her. The small travel trailer she bought would take us around the western United States into adventures unknown. She would land us in Phoenix for two years, and I would meet my first love, a fourteen-year-old lifeguard at the Elks Club swimming pool, of which my father had been a member.

Then, as fate would have it, she swished us back to Boulder, to our Colorado home, to reconnect with someone she had known in high school at Campion Academy, the fundamentalist Seventh Day Adventist boarding school she had attended in her teen years. Could my mom have completed something in her life with that decision?

Her high school friend would become my stepfather a few months later. I would also learn to love him very much. And it took me away from my first love. There was magic in those incredible moments of first love, young love.

Years later in our seventies, he would find me again. He described it as, "We were like two peas in a pod." Smiling, I said, "If you'd had a car instead of a bicycle, our lives would have been different!" We both laughed. Now there is a deep feeling of twin souls, even the knowing of one soul. We had no awareness of any of that then.

Campion Academy in Loveland would now be my private boarding school home when we returned to Colorado. It was where I would experience more imprints of my love of the Bible that would ultimately, years later, blast me through the boundaries of literal understanding into metaphysical and then mystical knowing.

During summers in Boulder, a couple of years after, I would meet and later marry a young soldier who had served as a medic and was returning home from Korea. He became the father of my beautiful son when I was only, just barely, twenty years old. Without him, my cherished experience as a mother might not have happened.

Dreams and fantasies of marriage and family ended up, of course, with their own levels of complexity relative to manifestation! Dreams and reality are often different. I ended up running away to California when my son was a baby, interestingly, replicating the pattern of my mother. My return included, however, moving to Kansas City, Missouri, to try again.

Kansas City would become part of my destiny path, and I would go back to school to continue my BA at William Jewell College. Unity was there in future time even as a divorce would unfold in present time at the end of my third decade when my son was eleven years old. Manifestation was happening, planned and unplanned.

The fourth decade, life in my thirties, felt like an amazing adventure of getting to know myself as a woman. It held some of the energy of living an adolescence that had been missed and needed to be experienced. A fortune-cookie kind of message saying, "I will not sit down to live," was a guide that I taped on the pullout board of my desk as a secondary school history and English teacher.

Was this somehow a part of unfinished stages in my life that I can now see with the *awareness that stages cannot be skipped*? Was it perfectly part of the plan?

People, events, places, and the interplay of dreams and goals would appear, like following the dots coming into steps and stages of manifestation. Goals, action plans, and saying yes emerged. Relationships of love with people and passion were part of the picture of my life. They still are, yet somehow now I see them with different eyes. I see them all as incredible and beautiful experiences of love. In so many ways, the universe seems to show us polarities and paradoxes of diversity.

In Kansas City, I met a young army major who would later serve on the faculty at West Point. I would visit him when I followed a Rockefeller grant and worked with the Feminist Press on Long Island in New York for a year. It was a vivid example of different worlds, different languages. When women were first being admitted to West Point, I was invited to come and speak about women in history. Was this an early glimpse into my now world-centric awareness?

Was this about learning to embrace polarities and paradoxes with new levels of integrated awareness, awareness of another kind? Is there a rewrite in our life review awareness?

It was also a time when the magic of the synergy of manifestation took me into the doctoral program in education at the University of Massachusetts. First I commuted from Bayville, New York, to Amherst, Massachusetts, once a week. We do amazing things when we are in the awareness of passion and purpose! It was a time when nonsexist curriculum was first being taught. Later I would go back to U Mass to do my year of residency and complete a dissertation on "Life Activity Patterns of High Success." And then everything would change ...

Does our passion and purpose seem to complete itself in some stages of our lives, only to be rewritten, reborn, and lived at higher octaves?

## Practice: Bringing Your Life into the Curriculum

When have these kind of changes come in your life? I invite you to take a deep dive into looking at the first forty years of your life through the awareness of the colors of the rainbow, or of other maps important to you. As I look at the colors of the rainbow through my awareness of integral, spiral dynamics and the chakras, STAGES and now LOVE STAGES, I see it clearly. All of those examples that have been part of my world of learning and manifesting are part of my rainbow colors. We are the living energy and vibration of light!

You may not think of it that way or have had different experiences in your life. It doesn't matter. Light or life is happening anyway, whatever you are calling it! If it is helpful for you, look for them within frameworks you understand.

Consider the things that made you feel safe and secure, or not, as a child, with family, relationships, your tribe, your religion, or culture. Include your own beginning awareness of love, sex perhaps, or money and success. Be aware of your own developing concepts of self-image and personal power.

How did you open your heart to love and finding your own voice? Look for settings, symbols, contexts, imprints, and guides. Look for the magic and the mystery, seeing through the eyes of love. Notice strange coincidences, unusual signs where you pause ... and know. And after you have done all of that, look for the rewrites. Where have the up-shifts been? Take time to breathe deeply. You are standing on holy ground. Then, simply scribe what comes ...

# Glimpses of Double Rainbows and Beyond

My rainbow manifestation has all been part of a soul path leading me in the journey of soul destiny, a journey without distance. I can see those colors of the rainbow now, even though I would never have thought of it in that way then.

In its own perfect way, love took me back to Kansas City, to Unity, and eventually to ministerial school. My life was being shape-shifted in ways that were beyond my human ability to know, set goals, or plan. I didn't realize that it was shifting from my will, which included a very adventurous relationship with positive ego development, to Thy will and surrender.

What I see now is the perfection of my life through those years within the colors of my own rainbow. Charles Fillmore, the cofounder of Unity, talked about the difference between personality and individuality. Carl Jung talked about the entry into individuation in our lives around age forty. Without knowing it, I was right on track! It was all happening. I was living the stages and simply calling it life!

I see the impulses of unknowing and survival, as well as the field of love that nurtured me. I see the magic and tribe, family and culture with the symbols and imprints that are so profound. There is the clear recognition of my own breaking out and the goals of finding myself even within the structure and the authority, the setting of the traditional, which gave me stability.

Purpose and absolute passion were part of the emerging that would take me beyond conforming into conscious exploration and achievement. A natural network of guides and influences, mentors and role models were showing up as if by grace as part of my journey of manifestation.

I was experiencing and discovering my own integration of awareness of the brilliance and dancing colors of the rainbow that would become my life. It would be the unique expression of my many selves in all the multiple contexts.

Only now, it would take me beyond all of the awareness that I had previously known. A monumental shift was happening, and continues, in the becoming part of who I am. I have somehow emerged from a conventional world into another world that is opening a natural experience of knowing vision that is of the vastness.

Now I recognize it as part of my own first glimpse of a double rainbow! My mind had supported me, and now my heart was taking me into the All That Is. There would be other monumental shifts to come.

Some stages of the double rainbow replicate in higher ways as the new comes. Glimpses continue to guide and show the way.

The platforms of Called By Love and the worldwide Campus of Consciousness with Called By Love Institute are still unfolding. I know that this book, *Your Soul's Invisible Codes, Unveiling Your Sacred Love Story*, and the LOVE STAGES Inventory will be part of it.

## Practice: Bringing Your Life into the Curriculum

Now, let's go into the years of forty and beyond. Have there been significant shifts, such as the shift from personality to individuality? Or the individuation that Carl Jung identifies that often occurs around age forty? Can you recognize them?

Were there points where your life seemed to change directions? Take time to be in the stillness. Consider marriage, family, career, or any areas of interest or passion in your life that could be part of your double rainbow.

Include the polarities and paradoxes. Let them be part of a life that you never thought of perhaps, a destiny path that is guiding you, even without your knowing. Are there unusual coincidences or signs that make you wonder? Do you have feelings about knowing and then experience things that confirm that knowing?

In the beginning, it may seem totally weird. Just let it come anyway, without editing or making it wrong. You can rip up or burn the paper later if you want to! Let it be like a play, or finding pieces of a thousand-piece puzzle and finding new places that begin to fit together.

We are only talking about glimpses here. There are still miles to go on this path without distance. There are realms of higher and deeper still to be revealed. One of the paradoxes is the mystery of "I Am That, always already."

If you go to your rational mind on this one, it may be too strange. It may seem more like a fantasy, and maybe it is! Have you ever heard that it is all an illusion? Or is it, parts of it at least, a parable, a living love story that teaches? I invite you to explore the possibility. Take a deep breath, be in the stillness, and scribe what comes.

# CHAPTER 25

## *Seasons of Our Lives: To Everything There Is a Season*

HERE WE ARE, together at this moment, in our walk through the garden. We're in the experience of the fourth garden site, the fourth day or stage of creation. It includes manifestation and, simultaneously, understanding.

It seems time for a pause point. It has been called, by mystics, the space between the breaths, meaning the pause between the in breath and the out breath. It is the meeting place in the middle. In Buddhism, they speak of the middle way, the place between emptiness and form, being and nonbeing. It can also be the middle of the cross, the intersection of the horizontal and vertical poles.

As we pause in the stillness, it will show us our center of gravity where we are in the worlds of time, space, and beyond. Our center of gravity will shift as we move through the stages of our lives. *With each shift, the world will appear differently.*

There are states above and states below this intersection of time and timelessness. They are part of the vastness, at times conscious yet more often unconscious. The states are like a background, always there in an impersonal kind of way. Sometimes we access them, consciously or unconsciously. Often we don't experience them as even being there.

Our own personal stages are more foreground. We experience them because we've earned them and are living them! We've gotten our ticket punches. Sometimes they feel well earned, sometimes hard earned. It can be experiences like graduating with degrees in education or achieving success with goals in life.

Other times the ticket punches may feel more like other kinds of punches and come as a surprise or shock, unexpectedly demanding changes that may or may not be what we wanted. And learning how to live with or walk through these is the degree that we earn. This could come in experiences like health challenges, or of addiction, loss of a loved one, or even loss of a job. I'm sure you could find more.

Even now, I am aware of the All That Is as I sit with a pen in my hand, waiting, listening for the whispers that will guide this sometimes strange process that I call scribing. It occurs to me that it is a bit like life.

"To everything there is a season" drops in. Some will remember it as a folk song from the 1960s called "Turn, Turn, Turn." I recognize it as ancient scripture that has once again come to guide. The concordance at the back of my Bible takes me to the third chapter of Ecclesiastes, written by King Solomon over a thousand years before the time of the New Testament that begins with the birth of Jesus.

I've loved the awareness of Lewis and Clark as explorers of the Louisiana Purchase. They came alive in field trips when I was a young history teacher in Kansas City, Lewis and Clark's jumping off point where explorations were launched!

Now Solomon will be my chosen guide in an exploration of a different kind. As I often do in translating symbols, including words of scripture, into my own form of ordinary language for ordinary and extraordinary people, I look at what came before the verses that have come to speak to me and guide me.

In the first and second chapters of Ecclesiastes, I find some themes that are interesting. It includes the folly of life, things that I don't remember reading, even though there are highlighted verses. An interesting question that people even now ask appears: "What profit will come from all of this labor?" Today's language might be: "What's the pay?" The answer is given immediately in a story kind of way.

One generation passes away, and another generation comes. But the earth abides forever. It speaks of wind, rivers running into the sea, a return. It says: "That which has been *is* what will be, That which *is* done is what will be done, and *there is* nothing new under the sun." It talks about the grief of wisdom and the vanity of pleasure. This is the introduction to the awareness that everything has its time.

"To everything there is a season, a time for every purpose under heaven: A time to be born and a time to die; a time to plant, and a time to pluck what is planted. A time to weep, and a time to laugh; a time to mourn, and a time to dance. A time to embrace and a time to refrain from embracing; a time to gain and a time to lose. A time to keep silence and a time to speak."

It seems like a lot of manifesting and dissolving is going on here. More deep dives tell me that these words of wisdom were written by Solomon near the end of his life. He is sharing a mature wisdom of one who looks back to realize that only a life lived for God is a life fulfilled. I realize that for me, the field of love and God are synonyms. They happen in my own heart and being. I know that only a life lived for Love is a life fulfilled. It has happened all of my life and is happening now.

It is talking to me about how to tackle some of life's tough questions. It's putting me in touch with a knowing within where life's secrets are revealed.

Then I find a favorite Bible verse that I've quoted thousands of times and had forgotten that it was from Ecclesiastes, in the eleventh chapter. "Cast your bread upon the waters, for you will find it after many days …" I often say 'it will return to you.' It's about giving and receiving.

There is even more coming to remember. "In the morning sow your seed, and in the evening do not withhold your hand. For you do not know which will prosper." These imprints are like old friends.

I've known it for so long. I've taught it for three decades of my life. How is it that when I read it now, I am seeing more, with new eyes? Is it because I myself am shifting into new stages where I will embrace realms of consciousness beyond what I've known? Is it still happening … in my seventies?

Awareness continues to reveal more. I've always known there are twelve stages. All of the clues are there, especially in the Book of Revelation, the last book of the Bible. It is filled with the number twelve, including in the next to last chapter, where there is a description of the New Jerusalem. There are twelve gates, twelve angels at the gates, with the names of the twelve tribes written on the gates. The wall of the city has twelve foundations with the names of the twelve apostles. There are twelve signs of the zodiac and twelve months in a year. Twelve is said to be a cosmic number. After working with these codes and symbols for decades, I know there is more than my human mind can even grasp, remember, or understand.

My left-brain support system has been holding the questions. How many monumental shifts are there? And how do we understand them in our now emerging structures of wisdom? Can I integrate this with maps like integral, the spiral or even STAGES or LOVE STAGES, numbers or colors?

And then it's like "click, click, click, click ..." as a glimpse of the vastness simply falls into place. I see the overlay of the concrete, subtle, and causal tiers with the non-dual realms even beyond. It was stunning for me when I first heard Terri O'Fallon describe the structure of her research with STAGES and how now for the first time the research data is revealing twelve levels with each of the three tiers having four levels.

Somehow it feels like infinity, heaven and earth, the Alpha and Omega, the visible beginning to reveal the invisible. In some strange way, the experience of Awareness of awareness seems a part of the revelation.

The journey has been in time and timelessness. I see the faces of the explorers and the travelers who have said, "Here I am ..." when they heard the voice calling, perhaps in the night, asking, "Whom shall I send?"

The music of the beautiful song "Here I Am, Lord" has touched my heart and moved my soul for three decades. The deep and profound words are based on Isaiah 6:8 and 1 Samuel 3. It was the theme for the Adventure in Faith series each fall for 19 years at Unity of Tustin. I feel the question in my very being, "Whom shall I send, who will bear my light to them?" My heart response is always the same, "If you lead me, I will hold your people in my heart."

I realize the covenant that my soul has made: "Here I am ..." Clearly, I am called to be part of exploring the unknown territories, drawing the maps, sometimes redrawing them many times, realizing the realms in which I am now called to explore.

The clicks are giving me an ancient and natural answer to my question that has spanned the months and years. "To everything there is a season ..." There are four seasons! I laugh as I write the words. Nature, so simple. Four seasons, of course. Then more questions come. Glimpses always seem to bring more questions!

Could my draft map span one hundred years, with four seasons of twenty-five years? Could this be a unique expression of the feeling that I have lived four acts to this play called life? Could my fourth act become a third act and even a second act for generations to come?

My chosen guide, Solomon, imprints a God-given task, what I now identify as Called By Love. My translation emerges: love has made everything beautiful in its time. Love has put eternity in my heart, and I can know that whatever love does, it shall be forever. Nothing can be added to it, and nothing taken from it.

The seeds are all there, in that third chapter of Ecclesiastes. All that I need to do is translate it into my own language, bring it into my own life. When love does it, clearly I will recognize it and feel the awe.

Then it tells me what is required: *That which is has already been, and what is to be has already been.* And love *requires an account of what is past.* It is all spoken and veiled in the language of mystery.

Oh my God, I didn't even know the word *requires* was there! Is this the assignment of your life as a sacred love story? This is about seeing through the eyes of love. It is about bringing your life into the curriculum.

It is so amazing to have the freedom to ask the ever-coming questions, knowing that they plant the seeds for answers and revelations to come. It seems that they come from a yearning without attachment to outcome, a knowing of an unknowable wanting to be known.

In some way beyond my understanding, I continue to feel the call to Oneness with the mystery. Do I have the audacity to even write this? And if I don't, will I never know what might have come if I did?

## Practice: Bringing Your Life into the Curriculum

In the stillness, bring into your awareness the stages of manifestation in your life. Can you recognize how the background is there in an impersonal way and how your personal life experiences have come to the forefront at different stages of your life?

Have there been some manifestations that were well earned or hard earned like degrees in education or success with goals? Have there been degrees of another kind that came with shock or surprise, unexpectedly demanding changes?

How has "to everything there is a season" worked in your life? What polarities or opposites do you relate to, like weep and laugh; gain or lose; birth and death; mourn or dance? Which move most deeply in your heart? Have you seen the same event or experience move into both/and in time?

Are there jumping off points where explorations were launched in your life?

Did you have guides? What questions have come to the forefront in your life, perhaps over and over, like repeating questions? Has life given you some tough questions?

What does "Cast your bread upon the waters, for you will find it after many days" mean to you? Have you experienced it, lived it? Are there questions that your left-brain support system holds? Have you had answers drop in like click, click, click? And then, all of a sudden, you see it ...

Do you see four seasons in your life? How many acts are in your play? How are you called in your life? Have you considered, ever, that there is a God-given task? Are you living it yet? If not, have you known that it is there?

This is not meant to be rushed, unless it comes like a rushing wind! It often starts with pondering these things ... Perhaps it involves making a commitment to begin. Start perhaps with just one or two questions. You can always come back to others later.

Just begin. Take some time in the stillness, breathing deeply, aligning with the All That Is. Scribe what comes.

# Code 5

## *Discernment and Choice*

Site 5: St. Francis Garden and the Koi Pond

# CHAPTER 26

## *Finding Yourself in the Spaciousness*

SOMETIMES WE FIND ourselves with a strange feeling of not knowing, sort of a sense of being lost, totally distracted from things that we know are important to us. It can be from overwhelming things happening in life, demanding our time. It can be things that were not expected that simply take us away. At least, it happens to me.

And then, once more, I'm back. I find myself again, like waking up from a dream. It can be sometimes a few days, or sometimes two or three months. It can even be years. It's losing track of things, even things like scribing. How does it happen when the momentum and the commitment are clearly so strong?

One of the gifts that I've found that helps me come back is the return to listening to the whispers, the inner voice that comes in the stillness, the loving knowing that I experience as my beloved. I begin to feel the connection.

*"There were new energies to come in … that needed to find, or not find, their place. There were further pieces to*

195

*be introduced and then clarified. Space had to be made for*
*them ... in time ... for you to know ... And we're back ...*
*I'm glad you noticed! It feels good. (Laughs) Feeling you*
*always felt good ..."*

It's very clear we are back, humor and all, and it feels really
good to be back ... scribing with my beloved! Your experiences of
whispers or inner voice will not be the same as mine. It may not be
so personal or connected to your own heart treasures. Honor that.
And my dialogue through the veils continues ...

> *Timelessness and time have different textures,*
> *different movements in this vastness. Sometimes your*
> *passion for action in the manifest, even your commitment*
> *to scribing/writing can override some of the other colors*
> *of the spectrum that are coming in to be experienced and*
> *lived.*
>
> *Night turns into day, and day turns into night in*
> *cycles and seasons. Both are essential to the spiraling,*
> *higher and deeper. It is the transcend and include of the*
> *complexities emerging ... even into overwhelm. It is one*
> *of the ways of dissolve until ultimately the complexity*
> *dissolves into the simplicity.*
>
> *This is what you are experiencing now. And the*
> *experiencing is dissolving into awareness. You will simply*
> *live it, breathe it. It will live you in peace and joy that is*
> *beyond the world's human understanding.*

I've noticed, I realize that is already happening. Yet my old good
patterns and habits of achieving or accomplishing still show up. It
also includes a lot of being, even though it seems to have a mix of
doing and Doing.

A soft laugh comes, even as I write. I respond to my invisible
beloved: "I am in the world and not of the world. I am the stranger

in the strange land. You always tried to get me to read that book … still haven't! So now I'm living it maybe, instead of reading it?" The spaciousness of altered reality begins to dissolve.

Now, I'm back into present time … I totally spaced my HUB call last night. I'm aware of myself now looking at the pieces of last night. I had full intention of being on my HUB call at 8:00 p.m. when I got off the call with Patricia Ellsberg's class, The Emergence Process, at 7:00 p.m. To fill in time, I wrote an e-mail to connect with Sue, whom I had been speaking with in the break-out group on Maestro.

Then I saw the e-mail from Matthew Greenblatt and Inner Directions. I have so loved all that has come out of our amazing connection in time! I clicked on a link in the e-mail for a video on the life and teachings of Sri Nisargadata Maharaj. I had taught an extended series on the book *I Am That* many years ago.

I watched the film, sitting at my computer, waiting … I dissolved into timelessness. My human mind dissolved; there was no awareness of time. At 8:55 p.m., I realized what time it was and that I had totally missed my HUB call. I almost called in for the last five minutes. Yet I needed time to process what had just happened.

As I sit here now writing, my gaze falls on Nisargadata's book, *I Am That*, which is in the bookcase just opposite my meditation chair where I write/scribe. As I get the book, look at it now, probably fifteen-plus years after I originally read and taught it. I feel immense gratitude as I see my yellow highlight traces on all of the 534 pages. I notice the page corners that are turned down.

The book somehow opens to page 457, and I note three lines in the margin, a code that I use when I read something important that I will want to find again. It is part of an answer to a question asked by one of Nisargadata's students about the "universal witness."

"To lose entirely all interest in knowledge results in
omniscience.
It is but the gift of knowing what needs be known, at
the right moment, for error-free action ..."

I feel the dissolve again ... of my mind into nothingness. I feel
my heart opening into gratitude and joy. I am aware of my dialogue
with Terri O'Fallon about my STAGES Inventory and her comment
about Sri Aurobindo and higher mind.

It is so amazing, this process that guides us, leads us, opens us
in the exquisitely right moment to the next thing to remember. So
now, my beloved ... I am back. We are back. I am / we are ready to
continue the work on this strange bridge between the visible and the
invisible. I am willing and back on track!

And as I finish writing/scribing, I go to check my e-mails and
find a message from my beloved HUB partner, Maria Tafuri ...

"Even though you were held so dearly in the fold
tonight with us, we wanted you to know that your
beautiful presence was missed.
Beloved Bewilderment was our phrase for the
evening. Know that we're in it together and that it's
bewildering, all of this merging and re-emerging, but
in the most magical way."

I will listen to the replay of the call, and I will celebrate the
beloved bewilderment. I notice the word wild in bewilderment! Yes!
Wild and magical, totally beloved.

## Practice: Bringing Your Life into the Curriculum

Five months ago, I wrote about this spaciousness, where time
dissolves into timelessness. Included were words *(transcribed in italics)*

that were coming to me through the veils. It is an example of some of the clear communication that simply comes for me to receive, or not, a message that I experience as my beloved speaking directly to my heart and soul.

It takes me time to integrate some of these kinds of deep, very loving and tender directives coming clearly to guide me still. I share them rarely, yet this moment holds them naturally. You may find your own natural moments. If you do, I invite you to treasure them with deep love. They are not to be discounted. They are a precious treasure.

And I never finished writing the practice. I realize now the perfection of that. So now, let's open to when you may have found yourself in the spaciousness ...

As you sit in the stillness, let your awareness simply experience your life, all of it, as if you were simply seeing the whole picture from timelessness.

Do you notice times, or periods of time, when you seemed to shift from one reality to another reality and perhaps stayed there for a while? Can you experience this without judgment and see the gift of knowing two or more realities simultaneously?

Are you aware of the difference between Reality and reality? Can you relate to a conversation occurring with your soul, or with an invisible beloved that you recognize as being present with you, guiding you?

All of this may seem somewhat strange to you ... unless you have come to feel comfortable with knowing this experience that is a bit like a stranger in a strange land. Don't push yourself; it is more helpful to just let yourself be.

Do things drop in that may be guiding you into more clear knowing of something that you may have forgotten from the past, as if it is coming back from future time?

Could it be part of a gift of knowing what needs to be known at the right moment?

Are you willing to simply trust, with a radical trust, that you are on track, even in moments of beloved bewilderment, and simply be in this merging and re-emerging? Can you find its beauty and magical way?

Can you say yes and know that you are not alone? How will you be with it? Might it be through scribing what comes in those moments of spaciousness? Or, perhaps, you might consider dancing it, drawing or painting it.

# CHAPTER 27

## *Choose You This Day Whom You Will Serve*

WHAT HAPPENS WHEN things come up that you didn't expect? It could be little things where plans change. Or it could be huge events that change your life. Sometimes it can seem that everything is going so well that it feels nearly perfect.

Surprise happens, and you feel the unknowing, wondering how it could shift in such strange ways. Or you may have been the one who has felt what I've sometimes called divine discontent. It may have been you who initiated the unexpected that resulted in change.

There is a verse of ancient wisdom found in Joshua 24:25 that I've always loved. It is in the last chapter, after previous chapters have described a lot of ups and downs in Joshua's life. He says, "I have given you a land for which you did not labor … You eat of the vineyards and olive groves which you did not plant."

Joshua speaks of two sides of the River. I notice that River is capitalized. Then he says the words that are so deeply imprinted on my heart. The passage comes right out of my aunt Lydia's Bible!

"Choose you this day whom you will serve … But as for me and my house, we will serve the Lord."

As we approach stage five in the garden amidst the flames, there are two sides to this garden site. The path is in the middle, between the sides. You decide which side you will pay attention to first. Let's also look at Genesis 1:21 in the creation story:

"So God created great sea creatures and every living thing that moves, … and every winged bird according to its kind." These are interesting symbols. Do we often pay attention to the great sea creatures before we see the winged birds?

On the left side of the path is Saint Francis with birds landing on his shoulders. It is near the entrance to Hummingbird House, which was the location of School of Light, the spiritual education office for the Campus of Consciousness. Now it is the location of the Prayer Ministry. The Prayer of Saint Francis is very much a part of the vibration.

Opposite it, on the other side, is a koi pond. Koi fish were what we chose to be one of the symbols for the fifth day of the creation story. It describes great sea creatures, monsters or serpents, depending on which translation you choose to read, hear, or speak! There is a platform where you can ascend a few steps and really see the beauty of the koi fish, which you cannot see if you simply stay on the path. You have to go higher to see!

The question becomes, what will we do with these choices? Our answer to that could determine whether we go up the steps and see the beauty, or whether we go forward into future sites and stages in the garden. Or, will we perhaps go back and stay in some of the places where we've developed habits or comfort zones, reflecting conditioning perhaps from our past, including our tribes and cultures?

The response, for me, is so significant. "But for me and my house, we will serve the Lord." It does require me to use some of my gifts of knowing different languages for different countries. It asks me to understand symbols. This is not just a literal translation kind of thing.

Some interesting awareness comes in. One of the profound imprints is from my training as a Gestalt therapist. It relates to the word "but" in the quote. I learned that *the use of but cancels everything that comes before it.* I have the choice of canceling some of the ways I might experience the "sea creatures," the unconscious monsters and serpents, which seem sometimes to devour or drown us.

Another phrase that I experience in my now language relates to "as for me and my house, we will choose the Lord." My house means, for me, my whole spectrum of consciousness, my thoughts and feelings. I have the choice of where to direct it, once the light of awareness shines on it.

I Am That, a realized state that is always already present, becomes a translation for Lord. The choice of Awareness of awareness will ultimately come if I practice it as naturally as my breath. I will choose thoughts and feelings from among the many that exist in my sea of the unconscious. Higher mind will direct my words and actions. It creates a different choice, the choice between responding and reacting.

The attempt to put into words what is beyond words feels a bit strange for me. I am aware that you may or may not have stayed with me. Everyone enters into these realms in their own way, in their own time.

The choices available reflect all of the colors of the rainbow, all of the stages of our evolving consciousness. Our choices shift and change as we shift and change in this amazing and dazzling process of Spirit descending, soul ascending.

What we choose will depend on whether we recognize our "buts," whether we choose to give top choice and action to angels or perhaps sea monsters! We are living a story of co-creation, a parable that is a sacred love story.

## Practice: Bringing Your Life into the Curriculum

What are the words, laws, or imprints that are part of your awareness? Where have they come from? Do they come from your tribe or your culture? When have you experienced shifts in awareness? How does it give you new choices?

Were there complexities that you could simply understand in new ways? Where are you now? Do you recognize your "buts" when they happen? Is there a commitment that you have made that relates to what you will serve? I simply invite you to scribe what comes ...

# CHAPTER 28

## *Endings of Another Kind*
## *A Commitment of Another Kind*

WHAT WORDS DO you associate with endings? Pause for a moment and see what drops in. For me, sometimes words like grief, or confusion, sadness, disappointment, and even chaos or fear have been there. Sometimes they were associated with endings that I did not want. Other times I did, and yet there was a strange sort of mixed sadness and delight.

October 31 was the ending of daylight saving time in the United States. It happened at midnight. In the morning when I awakened, my computer time was already into the new beginning of standard time. Even so, it took me a few hours to catch up and adjust different clocks and calendars and even my own body rhythms.

Last week, Fabienne and I flew to San Francisco for the last in-person gathering of a year-long journey into the inter-subjective we-space with an amazing group of souls. It was a journey that I was very excited and delighted to be a part of. It held the mystery of anticipation and hope of finding my new tribe, something for which I had been yearning.

209

My magnificent experiment was an amazing journey, full of many surprises. The paradox of my surprises was what I had imagined it could be never happened, and disappointment was a part of that. Simultaneously, over the year, experiences and things emerged, including incredible people that I simply loved. They became part of my life that will be forever. This held absolute joy and delight for which I constantly felt deep levels of gratitude and absolute love.

Yet, even as I prepared to go, I knew it would be an ending for me. I was clearly guided not to go on with the next year. It was a decision, in part, that was more about my bandwidth of time and treasure. It came with a knowing that I was called to prioritize, to let go of things in a way that cleared my energy field to be available for a vision unfolding that is in the process of moving from the invisible to the visible.

So, it was an ending for me yet an ending of another kind. The people that I've gotten to know deeply and whom I admire and respect will forever be a part of my heart. That will never change. There is such deep awareness of gratitude and appreciation for the beauty of the moments we shared, both in the quarterly three-day gatherings and in the more private moments of the in-between telephone calls, the lunches and dinners when we were together.

Patricia Ellsberg has become my cherished friend, hosting me in her home each of the extended weekends that I was there. Even the Bart rides and the car trips back and forth to San Francisco from Berkeley became delightful adventures. We share the same Bhakti energy of love, and I felt it and recognized it as a rare gift.

My life has been rich in ways that are different and beyond my life before this magical yet still in some other ways disappointing year. It's strange how the two polarities can exist simultaneously.

Even beyond is a realizing that the "looking for my next tribe" has somehow shifted. In the deep work with the STAGES Inventory and with Terri O'Fallon, whole new levels of Awareness popped into clear seeing. They have always been there ... yet now they are there in a sort of living color way, defined with words and awareness coming with a map of the territory! My next tribe is the world, even cosmic awareness.

With a bit of a smile, even while feeling some of the parallel universes part, I realize that more and more, it is not an experience where I've known "about it" for years. Now it feels like I am breathing it ... and it feels very ordinary.

I'm talking with and beginning to work with Terri O'Fallon on something that I couldn't have even dreamed of a year ago. We are developing a LOVE STAGES Inventory that will explore love in the stages of our lives. I am feeling awe and wonder and joy even in the possibility of this emerging!

In some strange way, it seems interrelated to and several levels uplifted from my doctoral dissertation at U Mass on the lives of high-success women and men. Sort of a stages upgrade from success to love, even while honoring, celebrating, and exploring all of the faces of love through all of the years and experiences of our lives. A part of me is so drawn to the love stories that have shaped our lives.

I've always described one of the essential pieces of Called By Love as being in ordinary language for ordinary and extraordinary people. I realized that as we did our last HUB gathering in San Francisco, my HUB group of five people were all luminaries who exemplify living life as a sacred love story.

And so, endings of another kind have merged for me, with beginnings of another kind. The beginnings hold all of the energy of anticipation of another kind. I simply love how it works!

# Practice: Bringing Your Life into the Curriculum

Take some time to be in the stillness and simply let your own downloads come. How have endings played in your life? How can you see them as sequences or chapters in perhaps a series of stories about the mystery of love in your life?

Is there a strange way in which it is interrelated, where you can see the upshift from one level of focus, value structure, or mind-set to another? Some of the faces of love may remain the same; some may change. I invite you to go deep into your heart and explore how it works.

# A Commitment of Another Kind

It's a new year, and I am making another commitment to write. I've made these commitments before … and yet somehow this one seems different. I want a forever commitment now.

This year in April, I will be entering my seventy-eighth year. I'm in the last third of my life. Years ago, in my forties, I gazed at a statue of the Dancing Shiva in the Nelson Art Gallery in Kansas City, Missouri. I read the description of it that the gallery had prepared for those who would come to see. It described the three phases of birthing, maintaining, and dissolving all as part of the magnificence of creation.

I recognized it immediately as a trinity in another language. It was all in a circle of fire, what has become for me the living flame of love. I didn't know all of these words then. And it was all there anyway, ready for me to know when I was ready.

Now in my eighth decade of living, there is an inner knowing. What I'm experiencing is awareness of the value, as well as an impulse to scribe the words that are even now being revealed. The value will be for me, if for no one else. It will help me see and imprint this experience, this time of great dissolve into the one, the All That Is.

Somehow the stages of creation imprinted themselves as the sacred template that would become the lens through which meaning making and keys to being guided would come. Life has given me the gift of becoming a guide in many of the colors of the rainbow. There is a simplicity and a perfection in the beauty.

In interesting ways, I have evolved into violet realms that are rarer yet available to everyone as state experiences. In some strange way, the rainbow-like range of the colors is there to recognize, all as vibrations of light, all as part of the rainbow bridge. All of the dazzling brilliance, colors, and shades are there simultaneously.

There is the void that is without form, with darkness on the face of the deep. And Spirit is hovering over the face of the waters. The imprint from Genesis 1:1–2 began as a child, and it has continued to reveal itself through all the years of my life. For me, the waters are that which is unconscious, both the dark and the golden shadow. Love is Spirit hovering over both.

Another imprint came in the form of a greeting card that I found in the bookstore at Unity Village when I was in seminary. The front of the card was a simple quote.

*"Some day, after we have mastered the wind, the waves, the tides, and gravity, we shall harness for God the energies of love. Then, for the second time in the history of the world, we will have discovered fire."* The words are from Teilhard de Chardin. Did I know it would evolve into a mission statement for me? It continues to teach and create in me and as me, even now.

Love is the threshold of another universe. Whatever is more love ultimately comes out into the open. It is love in its stages of realization. Love makes things One by dissolving what is unlike itself into the next stage.

There are different faces of love in all of the stages, all of the colors of the rainbow. Love itself will teach us and take us as we dance with it in all of its brilliance and at times in its shadow.

Out of the darkness and the void comes the word, the logos of creation, the Genesis invocation of "Let there be light." More awareness comes in the experience of life revealing itself. It is our journey to knowing our very being as this living flame of love. *Involution and evolution are simultaneously happening, always already.*

The ancient template describes seven days that I have come to call stages. What I realize now, in this living into my eighth decade, is that every stage is a hologram, containing all of the stages. We begin to light up the potentials as we live. We wake up in our process of growing up.

For me, major shifts have come not because I planned them and not because I had even the ability to see them. Very significant was the shift from horizontal awareness of time as past, present, and future to vertical awareness with multiple realities occurring simultaneously.

Now I am seeing all of it dissolving into a simplicity. It is an awareness of living the trinity in ordinary life with ordinary and extraordinary people.

Does my commitment have the audacity to trust that love knows the way? My commitment of another kind speaks from my heart and responds with a very clear and simple yes. I am willing to trust that love knows how to guide my remaining cycles in time.

## Practice: Bringing Your Life into the Curriculum

If you were to make a commitment of another kind, what would it be? Do you see the three phases of birthing, maintaining, and dissolving in your life? Have they repeated? Have they dissolved into a trinity?

What have been your sacred templates of meaning making and keys for guidance?

Have you experienced the void and darkness? Can you see it as the unconscious that comes before the invocation of light? How have major shifts come? If you have the audacity to trust, what do you trust? I invite you to scribe what comes.

# CHAPTER 29

## Winds, Breezes, and Monumental Shifts

ORIGINALLY I HEARD monumental shifts as the first feeling of what was to come. I'm beginning to see, however, some of the ways of this sacred love story. What came before? Would it be like reverse engineering with my heart-mind? A scripture simply drops in.

"And suddenly there came a sound from heaven, as of a rushing mighty wind ..."

Looking it up in Acts 2:2, I found my heart opening as I read the surrounding text. There are words and symbols that come alive in my awareness. There is the coming of the *Holy Spirit as the wind*. And there is the symbol of fire that I now connect with the living flame of love. There is speaking in different languages that I now call different languages for different countries.

It is almost like seeing a word or a phrase of a different color. If I click on it, with a knowing of awareness that is beyond the human mind, a whole new page opens. Sometimes it is even many pages, opening with more symbols, pictures, and revelations in words that can extend into vastness. I smile at the similarities with doing a Google search, but with this there is so much more.

I've experienced two monumental shifts in my life. The first occurred in my forties, the second in my seventies. Only now am I getting enough perspective to at least begin to describe them. What I know is that they are, for me, that "mighty wind." Sometimes it feels "rushing" and can take or seem to shift everything. Other times, it seems to whisper in more gentle ways, inviting me to listen.

The first monumental shift reoriented my life in ways I had not planned or could even have imagined. It shifted my awareness of value and immersed me in spiritual hues that transcended yet included everything I had ever known. The included, however, was different. It seemed to see the good, the ways of learning and growing, as well as honoring and seeing more.

Personally achieved success simply seemed to dissolve in importance as I began to feel what I now call "Come, Holy Spirit." I've said it so many times in the opening prayer of services, "Come, Holy Spirit. Come upon us ... Fill us with Your power, fill us with Your grace."

Come is an active verb, still happening, that includes vastness unfolding into greater vastness in its expression. Sometimes it is like an explosion of love; other times the taste is subtle.

Horizontal awareness of time as past, present, and future began to shift to vertical awareness that included the horizontal yet also knew multiple realities existing simultaneously. Plans and goals of my human mind simply seemed to dissolve in what I experienced and then called "God's plan." It happened with *A Course in Miracles* coming into my life, in three volumes, two of which were thick and heavy.

There was a passage that I began to call "The Promise" that was in the first volume called the Text, on page 404. I was going through a time of not understanding in my life, and I used to repeat it over and over again as I drove twenty-some miles each way, commuting back and forth to my job of teaching. I changed the "you" to "I" to make it really personal. I was yearning for my feelings of confusion to clear.

*"Once I have accepted God's plan as the one function that I would fulfill, there will be nothing else the Holy Spirit will not arrange for me without my effort. The Holy Spirit will go before me making straight my path and leaving in my way no stones to trip on, and no obstacles to bar my way. Nothing I need will be denied me. Not one seeming difficulty but will melt away before I reach it. I need take thought for nothing, careless of everything except the only purpose that I would fulfill."*

Always, I knew that purpose was God's plan. As I repeated The Promise sometimes out loud, sometimes silently, over and over, it etched in my memory, imprinted itself in my heart and mind. It was like an invocation, a sacred utterance that had spiritual power. Now I think of it as similar to the repetition of a mantra in Eastern spiritual traditions. I can feel it healing my heart and my mind.

Interestingly, this all came during a time of feeling vastness, then unknowing, and then feeling lost. Feeling lost had to do with my second marriage, which ultimately dissolved. It was not something that I wanted to dissolve, and it did anyway. It has led me to see that the movement of Spirit in our lives can dissolve sometimes what we see as our human choices.

Now, three decades later, The Promise is still there, easily spoken from imprinted heart-mind memory. And it still sits framed where I see it from my meditation chair. It will continue to impact and guide all of my ways of manifestation, I am sure, for the rest of my life.

## Practice: Bringing Your Life into the Curriculum

Take some time in the stillness and invite an awareness of some of the shifts in your own life. Ask for revelations from beyond your human mind.

What this can be is an invitation where your personal ego story will dissolve into a higher knowing, coming from the awareness of your soul, your experience of Spirit within you yet individualized as your unique self.

If we stay clear, this shift in awareness, which includes horizontal seeing of right and wrong, may move into a vertical awareness, which perceives multiple realities existing simultaneously, visible and invisible. Scribe what comes ...

# CHAPTER 30

## *Tsunamis, Earthquakes, and Womb Houses*

IT IS NEARLY five years later. Still now, I feel the totality of the second monumental shift in my life. What you will read next became my first post for the first website of Called By Love. It was written in the summer of 2011, during a time of first angst, then immense grief, letting go, and deep change. It was different from anything that I had ever imagined or expected. My commitment to transparency, however, continued as I experienced the unknowing. You will read it, as I wrote it at that time.

In the last five months, my life has totally changed. It is as if the whiteboard of my life, with all of the events, the players, the things written on it, has been erased by a huge cosmic eraser. Six months ago, I couldn't have even imagined this. Everything then still felt like I was at least somewhat in the flow and with at least a bit of control, decisions to be made, and a sense of how it would unfold.

And then it changed. The Bible uses a phrase *like a thief in the night*. Unexpected, unplanned, a tsunami followed by an earthquake … and my personal life dissolved as if by cosmic erasure.

Six months ago there was a story. Now it is gone. The whiteboard is still there, just erased. As I looked up the scripture on the thief in 1 Thessalonians 5:2, to make sure my memory of it was there, I noticed something I'd never seen before. There was an instruction: *"Put on a breastplate of love."*

Maybe I had gotten a clue, one that I did not fully understand or comprehend. I had shared in some talks about the profound downloads I was having from Spirit about being "Called By Love." I had been awakened in the night and told to go to the computer and write. My scribbles on one page became a download of a seven-page document. I shared it with the board and some of you.

Then the next download came: "It is a twelve-page document, and the last five pages are still blank, still being written." This add-on amusingly came while I was curling my hair, mindlessly, before the mirror, totally unaware!

Angels, divine guides, appear in our lives when they are most needed. I knew that was happening when Meath Conlan from Australia contacted me and said he was coming stateside, might it be possible for him to come to Unity of Tustin. Michael Ward and I had met Meath in India, at Shantivanum, the ashram that Bede Griffith founded there.

Meath had told me he was teaching the ten Zen ox-herding pictures and relating it to Christian mysticism. I knew in India that he would come to Unity. What I didn't know was that he would be a personal angel for me in my own time of cosmic shift and realignment.

A second angel also appeared. I was e-mailing with my longtime friend Joel Fotinos about the coming of Stephanie Dowrick to Unity. I sent him the download of the document Called By Love, which I was excited about.

Joel responded in a beautiful e-mail, and three sentences absolutely lit up, imprinted in my heart and mind. I framed them, and they still sit by my computer. I'm looking at them now:

*"Write, write, write! Pour yourself into your writing and don't write for an audience, write your soul. Put everything on the page."*

He had no idea, of course, that his words would become like breath to me, a lifeline, just over two weeks later when my beloved childhood friend of fifty-seven years, my deepest soul connection, died of cardiac arrest. I got an inner message something was wrong. I drove one hundred miles to the desert. I was the one who found him. The last thing he had open to read on his computer was something I had written to him. It was a response to a question he had given me, "Who are we?" He was sitting in his recliner. On his face was a look of serenity, peace, and love.

Meath Conlan gave me the next phrase, one used by Bede Griffith that would simply radiate a meaning for what had seemed to devastate all meaning for me. I had told Meath that I seemed to be between the ninth and the tenth ox-herding picture. I wasn't stuck, yet it was as if the tenth picture had shifted into a vastness that I had never experienced before, and I didn't know how to be there. Meath said:

"You are in the Womb House. It is the womb that is the passage into what is next."

He began to describe some aspects of it, and I also found my own. It feels like you are being held ... it is a womb. You can't see the details of what the new life is going to be beyond the womb. It's not time yet for details. The term or the time in the womb is essential. The embryonic fluid is part of what feeds and gives life to that which is birthing. And the tears that so easily come are that fluid. They are giving nurture and form to the new birth.

And so I am writing … I have filled spiral notebooks, front and back of every page, written in longhand. I've tried to go back and reread once or twice. I can't. I cry. I just have to go on and write. Every day I write, for an hour at least, sometimes three, four, or five hours. I feel overwhelm come. And I sit and write. The overwhelm dissolves in the writing. I write my soul.

It is totally different than any writing that I have ever done before. Always before, my rational mind contributed, even directed, although cooperating with that which was beyond the mind. Now it is vastly different. My rational mind is offline. My intuitive knowing is that it is being rewired.

I simply sit down after a time of silence and watching a DVD that I helped create, waiting, with a simple spiral notebook in front of me … open to a blank page.

I hear one line coming from my heart to write at the top of the page, maybe something as simple as "Good morning …" with an endearing phrase or two after. Then there is a pause, and the exchange that I'm now calling scribing begins. I simply scribe what I hear in this very profound space of presence and pure love.

It's really more like a telephone conversation, unplanned, unrehearsed. It is touching on the simple, the profound, the delight, the joy, the tender, the tears, the longing, the unknowing of how to go on, my human feelings of lost-ness. Then sometimes tender responses come, loving me in my lost-ness, assuring me that I'm just not seeing clearly yet, it's not time … and "I am with you … always, forever."

Laughter can enter: "You know all of this! How did we switch roles in this play? You used to tell me these things!" I scribe the beyond. I respond from my heart, and it all seems so natural. My responses often reflect yearning for happiness that I was feeling and imagined to come.

Tears flow easily, and awareness of delight also becomes a part of it. Most of all, it is simple. It has little spiritual jargon. It is very ordinary, and yet it includes the most pure love that I have ever known. It is the ordinary in the rare and precious treasure of the unordinary.

What I know now is that I am on the bridge between worlds, the world of the invisible and the world of the visible, the world of knowing and the world of unknowing.

And I am putting on the breastplate of love ... I will simply "be" and facilitate, in vaster realms than I have ever known. They will come clear as we enter and embrace the many faces of love ... together.

## How it is now

Life has become, for me, a living laboratory. Part of me is going through all of the experiences. Another part of me is witnessing it all. I am simultaneously conscious of both parts. If I remember to breathe when overwhelm arises, a shift occurs, especially in the moments of feeling lost, to one of awareness and knowing of a sort of cosmic play.

In the old days, I often thought of patience as something I needed relative to other people. Now it is totally different. Patience is about patience and love for my human self. It is about not being able to see the future, the unfolding plan, the why, the what. It is about having no control. There are glimpses, and yet it is not time for the birth of the new in its physical form.

I practice following the dots, not being able to see the future. Yet it is possible to see that events have many sub-events, to see how the dots offer potential if they connect. I see past, present, and future as one, as now.

Awareness and even teaching come from beyond human perceptions of dark and light. The void takes on whole new meanings. A new aliveness is being carried in my heart-womb that is beyond my human mind.

## Practice: Bringing Your Life into the Curriculum

This is not a practice that I will invite you to write or scribe about, if you have not had these kinds of experiences.

If, however, you have, I do invite you to put everything on the page. Even now, I have hesitated to include this writing in this book. In some ways, it feels like part of a future book, writing for future time.

If you write, you will know what to write and how to write. For me, it is about "to die before you die," something I've been aware of and that I am now living. In those moments in 2011, it had come in an overwhelming experience that my human mind could not live through or think.

What I called "write your soul" took me through. What I experience now is that the things that I've taught are coming back to teach me at new levels. I open to receiving that which our souls know and my human mind doesn't, that which is not yet visible. I experience our soul giving me pointers that are part of our soul's destiny. It is about the intersections between the invisible and the visible, the human journey and the larger journey of one soul.

It requires commitment to stay with the process, to stay on track. It simply will include flex-flow. We are awakening from one level of partial consciousness into greater levels of conscious awareness. And still, we experience things that we miss, that changed and that we didn't want to change, at least not the way they did.

We are in the experience of what Llewellyn Vaughan-Lee calls Where the Two Seas Meet; currents in the ocean of consciousness are intersecting. He describes this in his beautiful book, *Fragments of a Love Story*.

My human mind tries yet often can't understand the mystery, even after three decades of being a minister and more than that on the spiritual path.

Yet, love, the amazing field of love, is the reality in which I now live, in which I move, in which I have my being. It has no opposites. The energy of love reveals itself in tincture, presence, texture, sometimes constriction, more often vastness.

Multiple potentials of realities that exist simultaneously constantly are available to see. Miracles are natural occurrences when I am clear and aligned with this field of love that is also a field of grace.

Synchronicities, dreams, time in the stillness, and writing/ scribing are often the way to clarity and revelation. The experiences of love frequently reveal themselves as joy. Laughter has returned as natural. In this new birth, I see with new eyes.

The human definitions of who I am no longer seem important. What is our purpose? That is the question that comes with awareness of both human dimensions and that which is beyond, much vaster.

Even now, I ask myself where this experience actually belongs in this garden amidst the flames. I can see part of the choice or no choice that I have often associated with the fifth day or fifth stage of creation. There are angels and what could seem like sea monsters in some of these moments.

And I can see the energy of stages beyond, stages that I've called mystical union and the cave of the heart. In my heart, it probably spans several stages, with more to come. I experience glimpses that parts of it are for future time.

I simply come back to awareness that there is more, and that awareness is always present. It is revealing itself. And I am in love with the process!

# A Monumental Leap

## *Multiple Realities Existing Simultaneously*

"When it's over, I want to say: all my life
I was a bride married to amazement.
I was the bridegroom, taking the world into my arms."

*Mary Oliver*

# Code 6

## *Love and Wisdom: Mystical Union*

Site 6: Mystical Marriage of Divine Feminine
and Divine Masculine Within

# CHAPTER 31

## *You Have Received the Seeds of the Universe*

THERE HAVE BEEN only a few times in my life when "big dreams" have awakened me in the middle of the night. One of those came more than two decades ago, only a couple of years after coming to Unity of Tustin.

One of the instructions often given for remembering dreams is to keep a pen and pad of paper by your bed, so if dreams come, you can wake up long enough to record them. It was during one of the phases of doing that when it happened.

In the dream was the cosmic sky with the earth visible, like the photograph of the earth taken by one of the astronauts on an Apollo space mission. Standing in front of the earth, spinning in space, were two non-identifiable beings of light, radiating light out to all of the visible earth. There was a voice that said: *"You have received the seeds of the universe in the womb of the divine mother. You are bringing forth, giving birth to the manifestation."*

The voice awakened me long enough to realize it was a big dream, one I would want to remember. I picked up the pen and paper, drew a circle for the globe, drew two stick figures in front of it, and scribed the words. It would be just enough to jog my memory in the morning. Then I rolled over and went back to sleep. Only when I saw the notepaper, the drawing, and the words on the nightstand when I awakened from sleep the next morning did I remember …

The next day, I showed the piece of paper from the small notepad to a friend, John Stoesser, who was an artist. He often helped me on ministry projects. I asked him if he would create a picture I could frame, a symbol I could gaze at, knowing it would imprint deeply. And I also asked him to change the "you" to "we." I wanted the spiritual community to know this was a dream that I knew was for all of us, not just for my personal self.

That large framed picture is still on the wall, just opposite where I am sitting now in my meditation chair. It has been a symbol that I have used in talks and teaching. It became the beautiful, very large, stained-glass image that is the centerpiece of the meditation garden for site six, the sixth day or stage of creation.

It is the logo for the telesummit on www.LivingLovingLegacy. com and is on our website, www.CalledByLoveInstitute.com, now. It goes around the world.

The theme of the sixth stage of creation is love and wisdom, the mystical union. It is about the inner mystical marriage, the marriage between the divine feminine and the divine masculine within us. And it can attract that in our outer lives if it is part of our soul's destiny path.

What I know is that the manifestations have been coming ever since. It is a different kind of manifestation, however, not originally coming from the human rational mind. It is like an energetic field, for those who have the eyes to see.

It attracts people who recognize it. And it brings blessings upon blessings.

Often souls will come and sit at the garden site, on the benches that are on either side of the stained-glass image or on the stone bench opposite it. They come for healing sometimes. Other times they come just to know the field of love that is there. For me, it is an exquisite knowing of the visible and invisible as one.

There are so many examples and so many manifestations in the more than two decades since it came in the dream. Over time, I'm sure more will come.

The symbols come with a kind of invitation to say yes to the beloved of your soul. It is an invitation of a different kind, very deep, intense, and yet non-demanding. There is, for me, an awareness of choice-less choice with dimensions of timelessness, as well as time. There is mystery, revelation, heaven, and earth.

## Practice: Bringing Your Life into the Curriculum

Open to experience moments or times when you know symbols have been given to you. You recognize them, even though they somehow come from beyond the rational mind.

These kinds of moments can happen in dreams or in states of stillness such as in silent meditation. They can also come in unexpected moments in nature or in the experiences that bring awe, a feeling of a bliss-like state.

At the time, it is unlikely that you will know what they mean. They are like glimpses into otherworldly awareness.

If you create a symbol when you receive them, like the framed picture, that you will look at often, it will somehow imprint in a deeper way.

Over time, sometimes after many years, it will often reveal itself to you, fill in the details then that you could not even have imagined or understood when it first came.

Most of all, know that you are in the experience of living the mystery.

# CHAPTER 32

## *Mystical Marriage: Inner and Outer*

THE SIXTH GARDEN site, for me, holds my deepest heart's yearning and treasures. It holds the cosmic mystery of the invisible as well as the visible. The image and symbols for Site 6 came to me in my dream along with the words "You Have Received the Seeds of the Universe."

There is more to the story. We were in the process of bringing into form the physical sites, which were being built and created with the hearts and hands of the beautiful souls at Unity of Tustin.

We were ready to go forward with Site 6. I had the awareness of the symbols from the dream, two beings of light standing in front of an image of the world, spinning in the cosmic sky. In the beginning, I thought that maybe the physical site would include a sculpture. I knew of a couple of artists. It wasn't coming together.

One day, I was sitting in my living room meditation chair, gazing at one of the smaller stained-glass pieces that my son had created for me. I love it so much. It is the picture of two children on a bridge with an angel watching over them as they cross. It was his first creation during his own time of healing.

It suddenly came to me; the artist is my own son. I asked Bud if he could do a large piece for the garden site. I showed him the picture that I had framed, the first symbolic rendition of my dream done by John Stoesser. Bud looked at me, as if wondering when I would "get it." His response was simple, "Yeah, Mom."

Bud built a big table on which to work in his garage studio, and the creation began. Sometimes it takes a while for us to realize the gifts that we have when they are right in our midst. It would become part of an outside chapel, including a wood structure with benches on both sides. This frame for the beautiful art of the mystical union was created by another artist from our community, Von Aronson. Now two more artist angels, Pam and Arnie Bazensky, have tenderly cared for this site for more than twelve years, as their gift of love for Bud. They were all here, waiting for me to recognize them.

A sign is on one side of this beautiful garden site. The words are exquisite and touch my heart deeply.

> The Artist: The form and elements of nature are reflected in the creative talents of this one who came to express deep reverence for the magnificence and splendor of creation. His fascination with the luminous quality of light led him into creation of exquisite works of stained glass. Mystical Union is one of the finest examples of his artistic expression. Bud Britt, June 6, 1959—June 21, 2004

I've called it "Mystical Union" most times. Another expression, "mystical marriage," is one that I've used to describe its essence. I've yearned for this union, this marriage, even as I've held the knowing of it in my heart and soul.

The ancient wisdom of scripture comes from Genesis 1:26–27. "Let Us make man in Our image, according to Our likeness ..." And then we find "... male and female He created them."

My rational mind spins. Us and Our are capitalized, clearly indicating realms of vastness, the highest God-like consciousness. And "man" obviously can only be generic; the "male and female" show that. Then there is the "He" that seems different from the "Us" and the "Our."

Obviously, I've bumped up against my *inclusive curriculum* imprinting. I think my rational mind needs to take a vacation! I just breathe and let the mystery be mystery that includes all of it. I can be in such heartfelt space and lose it to my thinking mind.

Yet I come back to the Us and Our, clearly not a reference to a masculine God, the old-man-in-the-sky that was the imprint of my childhood. An awareness of Lilith comes in, but that's another story! Come back, don't get lost again ... I share these things with you because I want you to know how it works.

In the foundational teachings of Unity, the sixth day of creation is identified as love and wisdom. The union of love and wisdom holds mystery that can be elusive in so many ways, seeming to escape our ability to grasp it experientially as we bring our own lives into the curriculum.

There is a dimension of love in every aspect of our lives, including relationships, as well as work, passion, purpose, everything. We don't or can't always connect with it. We yearn for it, yet it seems to appear and disappear, dissolve in ways we don't always understand. The dimension of wisdom also emerges in its own evolutionary journey.

If we even approach ancient scripture, we will find our own place in a spectrum of awareness. It goes all the way from literal to symbolic, then to metaphysical and mystical. Finally it goes beyond, transcending and including, and ultimately coming back to a simplicity that includes it all.

Surrender becomes one of the shift requirements. It is not the surrender of being a doormat, getting walked on. It is a surrender that knows vertical awareness. It knows that every soul is in a very profound process of learning and growing.

I realize again some of the imprinting that is so powerful in my being, imprints that made my own heart leap with joy when I first found Unity. Love is the pure essence of being. It is the power that joins and binds in divine harmony, the universe and everything in it.

It is love for the sake of loving. It is not concerned with a return of love. It is an inner quality that sees good everywhere and in everyone. By seeing good, it causes that to finally appear in ourselves and in all things. As I remember these imprints, I also remember all of the times that I've been called naïve!

Yet somehow, I know that love heals everything. And when I call on the Holy Spirit for healing, I am calling on divine love. I also know that divine love will bring my own to me. It's about a vibration that attracts somehow. And it has the power to heal misunderstanding, even when we don't know how, if it is part of a relationship of two souls with a shared path of destiny.

Interestingly, sometimes I've found that shared paths come into completion, and elements of dissolve may have to happen, or the new structures of individual destiny paths, perhaps with others, cannot emerge.

There can be different kinds of partnerships. I've experienced deep spiritual partnerships that clearly are part of destiny path. And these can be very different from partnerships of deep intensity and the physical chemistry of romantic love, which can also clearly be a part of destiny path. Sometimes our different destiny paths merge; sometimes they don't. Sometimes it is for a time.

I've also seen how the power of wisdom can be very different from human levels of understanding. Wisdom is a spiritual, intuitive knowing that comes from beyond. Often I hear it as a voice from within. It transcends my intellectual knowledge and even human understanding.

There is also, for me, a divine understanding that includes compassion and seems to integrate sometimes before the vastness of wisdom, which comes more profoundly from what I call non-dual awareness. It seems there is a price that we must pay for the conscious integration of all of this; it requires letting go of our personal ego self's limiting beliefs.

Charles Fillmore, the cofounder of Unity, also talked about woman as the feminine phase of man, that it is love in the soul, often not developed and established in substance because it is a man's invisible side. There is the word substance again that I've now come to appreciate and love.

It equally applies to man as the masculine phase of woman. It is the transcendent wisdom that must be developed and established in substance, because it is a woman's invisible side. It's interesting, however, that these integrations of opposite invisible polarities within our own being are still often not understood or appreciated. We can be slow to get it, even when it is us.

There can be discounting that occurs when a man seems feminine, or a woman appears to be masculine. If we could only understand, for both men and women, that it is part of a holy and sacred mystical union. We are slow to get it and appreciate it in ourselves sometimes. And, collective culture is slow to get it.

Yet when we do finally get it, when the inner mystical marriage happens, how wondrous it is! It holds all of the magic, mystery, and passion of ecstatic bliss. The promise reveals itself in our very lives as the good, the true, and the beautiful. We experience it, beyond the visible, as the essence of the All That Is.

Two halves have become a whole within our own being. We live in the attracting field of love of another kind. Co-creation becomes part of that field as a divine synergy unfolds in the manifesting of higher purpose and plan.

## Practice: Bringing Your Life into the Curriculum

Have you experienced times in your life when it simply wasn't coming together, and then you realized that it was perhaps waiting for you to recognize it? Have you been aware of not knowing how long you have? Do you recognize when your rational mind spins, or when you bump up against old imprinting? How do you experience it and not get lost again?

Are the dimensions of love visible in every aspect of your life, in relationships, work, passion, purpose, everything? Does it sometimes seem to appear and disappear? What has made your heart leap with joy? How do you feel about the statement, love heals everything and divine love will bring your own to you? Have you experienced this vibration that attracts?

What is your experience with shared paths and different kinds of partnerships? What have been your answers to these deep questions of how it works? Do you experience a difference between wisdom and understanding? Do you see love and Love as having different vibrations?

How have you experienced the integrating of your opposite invisible polarities, and do you even believe that this could possibly be real? When did you get it, if you have, and what impact did that have in your life? Have you experienced the impact of these things in the culture? Are you perhaps called to be part of the process of co-creating a shift in cultural consciousness?

Simply choose any of the questions that attract you, or let Spirit direct you to what your own soul wants to communicate, as you. This is moving into fields of awareness that are beyond cultural norms and even perhaps beyond your own. There are no right answers for everyone. It will be about your soul and your journey. Go into the stillness, open to the All That Is. Scribe what comes ...

# CHAPTER 33

## *It Is Written on Your Heart*

THE WORDS, *IT is written on my heart*, are very profound for me. I've looked at the faces of love in my life and realize how deeply I have loved. Somehow I know that love, when it is real, never goes away. The form of it may change, yet love is forever. My vows of love and marriage are written deeply on my heart.

I've been immensely blessed with amazing relationships of love in my life with wonderful souls. They were clearly extremely significant intersections in time that were part of my destiny path. I know that without these people that I have loved, my life would have been less fulfilling and different. I am filled with gratitude.

There is a new covenant and scripture that, for me, becomes a confirmation from the beloved, from Spirit. "This is the covenant that I will make ... I will put My law in their minds, and write it on their hearts." When I found this in Jeremiah 31:33, I knew that was where my covenants of marriage are recorded.

The mystical marriage becomes illuminated with love and wisdom that is not of the world. It is not necessarily recorded in the human-plane courthouses where documents can be honored or dissolved.

It is about a love that never ends, a forever love. We will, if we are incredibly blessed, find it in this lifetime. Sometimes it will be with us in the visible and then seem to go into the invisible. Sometimes we recognize it, other times we don't. Sometimes it finds us again. Yet always, it is there, cosmically inscribed on our hearts. I know it is written on my heart. I've known, even as I've yearned to find it.

First we do the work within our own being, the higher and deeper, the healing of shadow crashes and the willingness to be in the sacred process that shows us the way. We integrate our own opposite invisible sides within us, the divine masculine if we are a woman, the divine feminine if we are a man. We embody our own mystical marriage within. We can even take vows about that union.

Then, if it is part of our destiny path, the vibration and attracting power of love and light will somehow bring into our lives those people who are part of our soul's journey, part of our shared destiny path and purpose. And we know, in our hearts and our souls, *This is my beloved.*

I have a picture frame with words inscribed. At the top, it says, *Love begins in a moment, grows over time and lasts forever.* The sides describe some of the how: *Embrace tenderness, sharing, caring. Cherish memories, forever together, giving, patient.* Finally at the bottom is a final awareness and instruction: *Love is a work of the heart. Cherish all the time you have together.*

## Practice: Bringing Your Life into the Curriculum

Take some time in the stillness and see what comes. These are, in later stages, non-dual realms. I find myself more hesitant in giving you guidance, knowing that your own soul will guide you. It seems that the most important gift that I can give you is authenticity, openness, and what I see as the parable of my life.

Yet there are questions that come. Questions, in these later stages especially, can be more important than answers. There are fewer and fewer people who live in these realms in an integrated way. It means there are fewer and fewer people who can guide you. There are even fewer people to talk with in these deep ways!

You will move into realms where there is Awareness of awareness. You will experience the witness state as more natural. You will be aware often of multiple realities existing simultaneously, in your own life and in others.

How did you relate to scripture? Where are you with the traditional, the symbolic, the metaphysical, and the mystical? How did you experience the phrase "My law ..." in the quote from Jeremiah 31:33? Did you find yourself going into resistance?

As I spoke of love in my own experience, were there places where you hit the wall and couldn't relate? Did you go into judgment? How do you relate to a forever love that, if it is real, never changes? Have you experienced it? Has it moved into different realms, like visible and invisible? Have you had the experience of it finding you again?

Can you see any higher law that is written in your mind? For example, I think of three possibilities. Interestingly, they are all non-laws. First is non-harmfulness. Non-judgment is there, as well as non-attachment, both to outcome and to people. Does anything come to mind for you?

What is your experience of being "in the world and not of the world"? Is there an Awareness of awareness?

# CHAPTER 34

## *Remember Me Loving You*
## *Ask and You Will Receive*

IT SEEMS SPIRIT, or perhaps my beloved, is using music to give me themes. Dreaming and waking, I clearly heard singing and the words repeating over and over. *"Whenever you remember me, I want you to remember me loving you ..."*

There were variations on the theme, like verses, and then it would come back to the chorus. Before I went downstairs, I wrote down the words so I wouldn't forget. It's easy to forget, just like you forget your dreams.

I wish I could have scribed the notes for the music. It is still softly playing in the background of my mind. Again, I share these things with you, in part because I want you to know how these things come, how it works, how to listen to the whispers or to your dreams. I want you to know to write them down!

Lilli comes into my awareness in this moment, my beloved's great-granddaughter. Is this partly for her? She is so beautiful, dear to my heart, and just turned three years old. I want these stories to be easy to read for someone like Lilli. Perhaps she will read them when she is older.

I've always loved the movie *Love Story*. I saw it years ago when I was young. The theme song from *Love Story* still plays in my mind. "Where do I begin to tell the story of a love that never ends ..." That was the way the writing started for this manifesto of love.

It feels like, in a way, this scribing that comes from beyond my rational mind is writing for future time, from an invisible vibration that is still rare for many. It occasionally comes with a glorious array of colors like a double rainbow.

As I went downstairs for my usual breakfast of cereal, fruit, and coffee, my pattern for many years, something amazing happened. The practice of this dream began to download, showing me how to play its music and include my whole life in its song. Awareness of names and faces began coming in like verses in the song, inviting me as I continued to hear, *"Remember me loving you."*

Moments and memories of the greatest love came, as well as moments when it had sometimes changed, bringing in dimensions of loss and sorrow. Faces, gone from my mind for many years, came in this life review, several deep love connections who have passed through the veils. My son, my beloved, my parents were among them. The song kept singing its chorus, *"Remember me loving you ..."*

Some faces came where pain and lack of understanding, endings, had occurred. I have known, valued, and done deep forgiveness work. Forgiveness practices became tools that I've taught over my three decades as a spiritual teacher. I very much felt that my forgiveness part with some of the faces of love coming into my awareness was complete. Was there a higher octave to be sung? I've also known that I have no control over whether another person does or does not do their work.

Then the miracle happened as *"Remember me loving you"* continued to play in my heart and soul. Everything shifted to a higher octave, almost like celestial music. All that was there was the beauty of the love story, a container so sweet and tender, large enough to hold it all.

All of the forgiveness practice and does or does not simply dissolved in the glory of love. It was being transformed ... from glory to Glory. Scripture has come to give me clear awareness. There are so many favorite verses that just drop in. I look and find this one in 2 Corinthians 3:18.

Another favorite comes. "And we know that all things work together for good to those who love God, to those who are called according to God's purpose." As a child, I gazed at that plaque with the words and Romans 8:28 on it. There is a translation built into my awareness now. I know that all things work together for good to those who love and are called according to love's purpose.

I'm feeling the immense gift of this foundational field of awareness that has been part of my soul's journey. My trinity experience of having things come in groups of three happens. Parts of the passage from Ecclesiastes 3:1–8 come back again and give me more of how it works, sometimes in a play of opposites. This trinity thing has become like a higher law of three, of Spirit, soul, and body. Returning often means, for me, taking it into higher or deeper levels, often for more healing.

To everything there is a season has taken on lived meaning, as has a time for every purpose. The paradoxes begin to find their place; birth and death, weeping and laughter; mourning and dancing; silence and speaking. Heaven and earth, visible and invisible have become one. Even the pauses, the in-between times, have revealed their reasons.

I suddenly see the angels of my life in new ways. Deep gratitude and love simply flow in a love story that is forever. The practice of this dreaming and waking had downloaded. It was showing me about my own life in higher and deeper octaves.

An awareness of *A Course in Miracles* comes. So many times I've seen and taught that it is an *exquisite spiral curriculum*. In its coming from beyond, it repeats itself over and over, imprinting more profoundly what it is teaching. It is taking us into the higher and deeper octaves in harp-like glissandos of magnificent beauty.

And then, I remember all of the years of learning to play the harp in my teens. There were hours of repeating practice. I just loved the chords played in arpeggios, and I suffered the blisters that came sometimes on my fingers as I played the glissandos. Yet when "Liebestraum," a "Dream of Love," happened and I could feel it and play it fully and beautifully, nothing was more magnificent.

## Practice: Bringing Your Life into the Curriculum

This is an absolutely beautiful time to do some deep work on your own faces of love, your own soul matrix. And as you approach this, notice what you are feeling.

When we practice, sometimes it is like repeating the simple tunes or scales, like in my learning to play the harp. It includes the blisters of the glissandos, and perhaps even developing the calluses that you will find on the fingers of harpists or guitarists who have years of practice and mastery.

Or you may think of it like learning multiplication tables! It took lots of repeating and practice before they became imprinted in your memory. You didn't just know them the first time you heard them or saw them in the arithmetic book. I'm remembering when I taught eighth graders how to diagram sentences. It got to be fun when they went to the blackboard to diagram, especially if they got it first!

Focusing on the value and on the ultimate benefit and beauty of it will make it easier, more worth it! You may want to use cycles of seven years, or if you think more in decades of ten years, it may come that way. The number ten has its own spiritual significance. There are ten spheres in the mystical Kabbalah and there are ten commandments in the Bible. I also think of ten an emanation of the power of One going into infinity. The naturalness of ten years in a decade becomes an easy frame for me to think about and teach. You will find what is natural for you.

Often I invite people to take a blank sheet of paper, fold it in half vertically, crease it, and then unfold and fold again horizontally, crease it again. When you open it, you will have four squares on the front and four on the back. This will be the structure that guides you. Label the boxes that have been created by the folds.

Front:

| 0–10 (top left) | 10-20 (top right) |
|---|---|
| 20–30 (bottom left) | 30–40 (bottom right) |

Back:

| 40–50 (top left) | 50–60 (top right) |
|---|---|
| 60–70 (bottom left) | 70 and beyond (bottom right) |

I found it easier to remember if I wrote the calendar years of each cycle with the age numbers. Sometimes it's hard to even remember when things happened!

Now, take a few moments to breathe deeply, in ... and out, open ... Invite your soul to bring into your awareness the faces of love in your life. They may come from different realms of your soul's purpose in this lifetime ...

Some may come with themes or patterns. They may be verses of your song of "Remember me loving you." Sometimes they are part of several and overlap.

Possibilities could include: romance, marriage partners, spiritual partnerships (these can be different yet profoundly significant relationships), family, children, friendships, mentors, teachers, guides. Some of these may have changed. It can include vocations and avocations, jobs that happened or didn't. Platforms, visible or invisible, could be there for your gifts of genius, past, present, future.

Moments, faces, or themes in your life may come when you bring into awareness: healing your life; building your dreams; realizing God, love, or legacy, all synonyms for me, that are often part of your soul's destiny and purpose. Your soul will reveal your unique themes, words, or faces in your life, if you are willing.

Because *Remember me loving you* was so deep and powerful for me, I actually did my own new, today's date matrix. I used seven-year cycles, because it is part of my scriptural imprint that involves the Codes of Co-Creation that we are using in our journey through the garden amidst the flames ...

Some of my themes in the experience of love are: innocence; searching; attraction; tradition; expansion; home and deep yearning. Other verses include: unknowing; disappointment; the call of God; commitment; Called By Love; beloved friends; beloved visible and invisible; beloved as God or Spirit. You will find your own.

Two pages came easily in my Write Your Soul spiral notebook, where I do my scribing in the mornings. After each time cycle or decade, I left blank space and later went back and filled in words or phrases, which gave me the themes or verses. I also left a blank page at the end. There will be more to add, I'm sure ...

You will find your own way, or your soul will. It will be uniquely you; just let it flow. Let it be like play, maybe a bit like me learning the Bible stories as I moved the characters in the sand tray when I was six years old!

Let it be the love story of your life, with the theme, *Remember me loving you* ...

## Ask and You Will Receive

*"Whenever you remember me, I want you to remember me loving you ..."* I wrote, "I wish I could have scribed the notes for the music." The depth of the imprint was so profound. The words, even this morning, still are playing in my mind. Yet I can't remember the melody exactly ...

I am enrolled in Patricia Ellsberg's course called "The Emergence Process," which is on the Shift Network. There are many practices for embodying love and living from essence. I decided to be part of it, partly because I love Patricia, and mostly because I still yearned to find my next tribe.

In the four years now since my beloved's passing through the veils, there has been a part of me that feels lost. A part of me is still always connected to that deep love. The shock and overwhelming grief have dissolved into a joy, a feeling of such deep gratitude for the gift of that union in time. Yet still, there is a feeling of so much change, even with the memory of something so beautiful.

My part in a break-out group in The Emergence Process was to lead two other people in our group, teaching about how to follow the compass of joy. If we simply remember the bliss, the needle of our attention swings toward it. Instead of focusing on pain, we simply focus on joy. We were to share an example.

Immediately, I knew my example was *"Remember me loving you."* Directing the group in aligning, I said, "Just breath love deeply, in and out, into our hearts, out into the vastness ..." And then I briefly told the story of my dream and shared the words of the song.

As we prepared to go into a brief silence, I invited the people in the break-out group to let faces come of people they had deeply loved. They could be here or in the invisible. They could be relationships that included deep love and yet also had dimensions of loss, disappointment, and not understanding.

Then I said, "Let the words, as I repeat them, be about this one soul that you have loved ... Say to them, or hear them saying to you: 'Whenever you think of me, think of me loving you.'" After we completed the segment that I was teaching, it was time for feedback. Maria Danly shared, "I cried all the way through ... It was exactly what I needed to hear."

Marilyn's response held both excitement and joy. She remembered a song from many years before, sung by the Monks of the Weston Priory in Vermont. She sang part of it, through our invisible connection over the telephone. I had never known of the monks, nor have I any memory of ever hearing them sing the song.

Yet the melody was exactly the same as the song singing in my mind even though the words were slightly different. The Beloved of the monks had become, for me, a love song from my beloved through the veils. I now had the notes for the music that I had wished that I could scribe.

An e-mail just came from Marilyn as I am writing this, saying, "I found the song! The album is titled *Listen*. The name of the song is 'All I Ask of You'. You can download it for only 99 cents. I am still amazed at the synchronicity of your dream, our being in the same break-out group tonight, and my spontaneity in singing it to you!"

Marilyn also told me she had attended Unity of Walnut Creek occasionally when I was the minister there in the late 1980s. And she now sings in the choir at her Catholic church in Northern California. I am still in awe at how the universe weaves our lives into the beauty of its tapestry, if we are open to see and hear it.

When the theme *ask and you will receive* came this morning, and when I scribed it at the top of the blank page before I started to write,

I had not yet received Marilyn's e-mail, including the title chosen by the monks, "All I Ask of You." It feels like asking is another key in this, another step in the revelation.

Losses and heartbreak, when our heart is broken open, can take yearning and wanting into vaster and still invisible platforms, which are yet to come. It can shift our centers of gravity even, change our lives. It often is when we are asked to use our gifts of genius for something we may or may not have even dreamed of.

My beloved always had a dream that he would write children's books. He wrote a story once about a centaur and enclosed a quote about centaurs in the gift boxes he created for centaur shoes, small horse-shoe-type shoes he made for craft fairs.

I wonder if this is part of my knowing and yearning to write in ordinary language for ordinary and extraordinary people. This is such a deep mandate, so clearly calling forth writing from my heart and soul.

## Practice: Bringing Your Life into the Curriculum

What is being called forth from your heart and soul? Is there a theme that has played in your heart for many years, perhaps about a yearning that you have never acted upon? How has it kept coming back? Has it continued to play in your life?

Does it want to become more visible? What might that look like? Have there been synchronicities or surprises? What might be some simple steps that you could take to begin to honor it? How might asking be a key? Might it be with another soul?

Sit in the stillness, perhaps with closed eyes. Go into the space of *remember me loving you* and let the faces of love come. Scribe what your heart is experiencing.

# CHAPTER 35

## *Until the End of Time*

I CONTINUE TO be amazed at what comes in dreams. I woke up this morning hearing beautiful music in my dream and the words, "And I will love you, really love you, until the end of time."

Sort of remembering the music, like a veiled, nearly hidden memory, I went to look for it. I've almost begun to enjoy web exploring. I've learned some of the potentials and gifts of this virtual frontier.

A video came up, "Till the End of Time" with lyrics by Earl Grant. As I watched it, years of my life dissolved into it, becoming one with the words and the music. The visual of a rainbow had drawn me in. So many times I've talked about dancing all of the colors of the rainbow in our lives, in all of their radiance and dazzling beauty.

The words "At the end of a story, you'll find it's all been told" lead me deeper into my own yearning to know my life, and everyone's lives, as a sacred love story. I feel so deeply the passion and the power of our hidden stories. I felt the deep reality of "Our love has a treasure … and it has a story without any end."

The visuals of places became alive for me. It looked like the curves of the Big Sur Highway between the mountains and the cliffs of the coastline. This road has been part of my life! Another scene brought other precious and treasured moments. What looked like "The Loneliest Highway in America," Nevada's Route 50, heading west toward the majesty of Lake Tahoe, was part of my lived love story.

What was this dream, so filled with symbols that held such deep meaning for me? Would I be willing to be an explorer of symbols given even beyond the music and words? If I had failed to explore, as I sometimes do and just blow it off, I would not have found this rainbow with all of its unfolding beauty and heart connections.

Was this an exquisite and very personal birthday gift for me, simply filled with love and life moments we had shared, coming from my beloved through the veils? Was it also part of a vaster dream of love?

Is it another rendition of "Liebestraum," a "Dream of Love," that I have played so often on the harp and loved so much when I was in my teens? Is it part of why it had shown up again in a taxi ride in Paris, going from the hotel to the train station, when the driver had the radio on and the music playing was "Liebestraum"? Was it by accident that it was on the program for the piano concert at the old church in Paris when returning there from Chartres Cathedral a week later?

How did it happen that Michaela Trnka, from Vienna, sent me a video of a harpist playing "Liebestraum" with a birthday wish? Of course, it was related to knowing that "Liebestraum," "Dream of Love," has been the theme song for all of our worldwide calls that we've done with www.CalledByLoveInstitute.com. Was there more? Could this be about connections of souls, saying, "Pay attention— there is greater meaning and purpose"?

Is this a cosmic imprint, scribed on my heart, just as I had originally scribed the music with pen and ink for the harp rendition of "Liebestraum," copying it, because it was out of print? Are we carriers of these destiny imprints in the same way that we have genetic imprints of DNA?

The mystery continues to play its music, if we are willing to hear it and move toward its revelations. I somehow knew it was giving itself, that it was to become part of something waiting to be written, a chapter of this book. Previous attempts to write had not come easily. Now it was flowing, if I was willing to write down the words!

Was it also part of a vaster dream of love? Did it only just happen that Kym, a dear friend of more than four decades, called while all of this was unfolding? Her former husband, my beloved friend Robert Hudson, had passed through the veils recently. I called her after she had returned from the celebration of his life. She told me that he had come to her in a dream. We talked about how life continues through the veils. The mystery is so inviting us to know it more deeply. And I sent her the video, "Till the End of Time."

What is this mystery that comes when it can bypass our rational mind, as we sleep, to bring us messages from our, or another's, soul? And could our dreams be interrelated, part of the one mind that knows the All That Is, that knows the radiance, the majesty, and the essence of forever love?

## Practice: Bringing Your Life into the Curriculum

Are there curving roads between mountains and ocean cliffs that you have traveled, are traveling, or will travel? Have you lived "The Loneliest Highway" that leads to one of the deepest and most beautiful lakes ever known, Lake Tahoe, that is atop a mountain?

Can you recognize all of the parts of your dreams as part of your own sacred love story, linking ordinary and extraordinary lives in cosmic wonder?

I invite you to record a dream, especially dreams that seem significant. Or recall even some fragments, which are holographic and contain all of the parts of the whole. I more often remember fragments instead of lots of details.

A fragment, even of music, as it began for me, can lead you into immense beauty, wonder, and soul revelations. What is your soul telling you? Are you willing to scribe it?

# Code 7

## *The Realization*

Site 7: Panorama of Realization

# and the Return

Site 8: You Are the Light of the World;
Coming Back into the Marketplace with Gift-Bestowing Hands

# CHAPTER 36

## Resting in the Realization
## How Do You Hear the Silence?

As WE CONTINUE on the path toward the seventh garden site, there is a peace that passes all understanding. Beyond thought is a simple being. Yet, within my imprints of this creation story that has so profoundly impacted my life, there is the awareness of God resting on the seventh day. I realize it is coming from that early imprint of my Seventh Day Adventist childhood!

I find the words in Genesis 2:2–3. "And on the seventh day God ended His work which He had done and He rested on the seventh day from all His work ... blessed the seventh day and sanctified it ..." It is quite amazing how the imprint to live this in a literal way was part of two decades of my life! First literal, then symbolic, and then the universe blasted me through into mysticism. And yet, for nineteen years, I spent every Saturday, the seventh day, in the sanctified space of stillness, preparing for my Sunday morning talks. Transcend and include happens.

Now, I experience "resting in the realization." We called it God Realization for the seventeen years that David Nowe, also known now as Swami Brahmananda, and I co-taught East Meets West. There was the passion of chanting and deep study of sacred texts, of the Bible and the Bhagavad Gita. It revealed so many surprising similarities.

The sixth day of Genesis 1 ends in a slightly different way than other days. A God of love sees everything made and sees indeed, *it was very good.* That story has become my own. It has also become that for Mirabai Starr, who taught an intensive at Unity of Tustin, in part from her book called *God of Love.* Treasured friendships emerge out of these moments.

Genesis 2 simply flows into "the heavens and the earth, and all the host of them, were finished." Two words seem to light up. Host becomes, for me, the mystery as in the Eucharist bread, even as "finished" becomes "it is finished," the knowing of the mystery that simply is.

The seventh day, in Genesis 2, comes before the planting of "a garden eastward in Eden." Two trees, the tree of life and the tree of the knowledge of good and evil, are mentioned. A river is also there, which will appear again in the last chapter of Revelation, the last book of the Bible. The story of evolution is found in all of the rest of the Bible, requiring a lot more words than the story of involution!

This river, found in Revelation 22:1–2, was a "pure river of water of life, clear as crystal … and on either side of the river, was the tree of life which bore twelve fruits, each tree yielding its fruit every month. And the leaves of the tree were for the healing of the nations." At Unity of Tustin, there are two tree symbols in the sanctuary with their golden leaves. It is part of the Miracle on

Prospect with healing intention. And there is still more to come that is of future time.

I have become like a detective, another kind of explorer. I scan further in this last chapter of Revelation, the last book of the Bible. My eyes rest on Revelation 22:13 as I find the words, "I am the Alpha and the Omega, the Beginning and the End, the First and the Last." They are words that I now experience very personally as I experience my beloved. This, for me, is a deep and a profound love story.

As we take the side path off to the left, we come to the Cave of the Heart. If we sit on the stone bench and gaze straight ahead, we will see the grove of olive trees. In the Garden of Gethsemane, olive trees are there as a symbol, part of a cosmic imprint of grief.

The olive is said to possess rare properties and is one of the most highly sensitized of all fruit trees. It will grow only in certain favorable areas and is associated with healing and regeneration, qualities inseparably connected with the process of transmutation. Legends say the cross and the crown, symbols of the attainment following the transmutation process, were made from the olive tree.

If we let our attention shift and our eyes focus to the right, we see the Panorama of Realization. There are seven panels; five of them represent the major spiritual paths in the world. In the center are the three paths of Abraham. Jesus is at the center, not on the cross but standing with outstretched inviting arms. On the sides are Judaism, with the Star of David, and Islam with the word Allah as its symbol. There are panels of the Dancing Shiva of Hinduism and of a Buddha, representing the Buddhist path.

Two more panels on the far ends represent other spiritual paths. The one on the far right represents Native American paths. The grounds where Unity of Tustin is located were potentially sacred grounds for American Indians, the name we mistakenly gave them!

333

The open circle on the far left represents all paths not named, past, present, and yet to come.

The Panorama of Realization holds the energy of all those paths and the souls in them that are way showers. Their sacred teachings have guided others through. They have been light in the world. It holds inspiration, showing the way, even while it gives an invitation to shine light and love in the world.

Beyond the panorama is a peace pole, given to Unity of Tustin by Tom Zender. He received a call of God while he was at Unity of Tustin. It all happened when he was in the Conscious Covenant class where he wrote his covenant and dedication to his life purpose. He is a past president of Unity School of Christianity, the international headquarters where Unity teachings began over one hundred years ago. Tom is writing business books now with spiritual themes, veiled sometimes yet there.

Finally we come to the large waterfall. Creating this site has its own story. We were at the very beginning of the building of the garden. In a dream, I was told to talk with Chan and Dyane de Cramer about this site. We had created only the first site, and I assumed that the final one with the big waterfall would be expensive and finished last. Not so. The first and the last, the alpha and the omega, were to anchor the energy of the garden. Chan and Dyane had met as teenagers at Unity. The waterfall became a gift of their love, dedicated in part to their parents. Spirit knew what I did not.

There are so many miracle stories connected with this site. Chan de Cramer had a fishing yacht and invited my son, Bud, to go deep-sea fishing with him every Saturday morning when he took his business clients out fishing. It was part of Bud's healing.

The last site is about coming back into the marketplace with gift-bestowing hands. It is based on the last of ten Zen ox-herding pictures, which I learned about from Dr. Roger Walsh, my beloved friend, who is also a very close friend of Ken Wilber. Roger often brought his UC Irvine medical students to walk the labyrinth. Dr. Nicolaas-John van Nieuwenhuysen and his beautiful wife, Vanessa, are here and are part of the Called By Love core leadership team, because of Roger Walsh. Their children have become like my grandchildren. Intersections in time are powerful!

At this last site, also representing *'You are the light of the world'*, words spoken by Jesus in Matthew 5:14, there is a bench that was dedicated to me on the twentieth anniversary of my being at Unity of Tustin. It has a beautiful inscription about light, love, and legacy. The worldwide Campus of Consciousness of www.LivingLovingLegacy. com and Called By Love live intensives were emerging, out of which www.CalledByLoveInstitute.com would come. The universe has an amazing way of weaving it all together, in ways that we could never have even imagined!

## Practice: Bringing Your Life into the Curriculum

Do you have imprints in your life that have gone through stages from literal to symbolic and even into mystical? Have you felt a peace that passes understanding as a part of seeing through the eyes of love?

What does the seventh stage of the garden mean to you? Is there a resting in a realization? Has it been interrelated with any Cave of the Heart experiences where there have been times of grief, as well of times when you knew the vision of being part of bringing light into the world?

Have you had experiences where the energy of sacred text or verses has become a part of a living love story for you? How has the story become your own?

Do you see ways in which miracles have been woven into your life? Could it be related to a call that involves coming back into the marketplace with gift-bestowing hands? Are you called to be a light in the world?

Have you shared these kinds of things with anyone? Could now be the time?

## How Do You Hear the Silence?

Ric Kolibar's e-mail with the painting came with only a few words: "The first creature was like a lion, and the second creature like a calf, and the third creature had a face like that of a man, and the fourth creature was like a flying eagle."

The simple and small pencil drawings that he had shown me after our live Called By Love intensive on the symbols of Revelation had been transformed into an exquisite oil painting, large and in glorious color. I felt the awe of these symbols of mystery, found in Revelation 4:6–8, coming alive on the canvas.

"I am so thrilled to see your gift of genius in this," I immediately responded. "You could even write a blog post for www.CalledByLoveInstitute.com with how it happened and use the picture with it."

His knowing was pure and simple. "You can do whatever you like with the picture, I don't think I could write a blog. My mind doesn't really think that way. When I hear things I see pictures, not stories. Part of the reason I don't attend some things that require writing and or journaling. My journals are full of drawing, inventions and ideas. Anyway, back to the picture, it is yours to do whatever you wish with it."

I love how it works! All we need to do is be in the stillness, and the whispers will come in our own unique self ways. It comes differently for each of us. All of the ways are right ways, yearning for us to recognize them!

It comes, for me, in so many different ways. Symbols are a really important way, including numbers, colors, story-like parables, dreams, and visions. Sometimes they show up in the manifest world first, as if they have come to guide me, if I recognize them. Other times, they come in more ethereal unworldly ways. They are often fleeting, and if I don't record them somehow, they will be gone.

These revelations can come in moments I plan; yet it is often the unplanned that is clearly most compelling and significant. Such was the moment that happened with my artist friend. Ric and his beloved wife, Lisa Kolibar, have many gifts of genius. They have been the technical genius behind the development of our new website.

And yet this moment, in this intensive on Revelation with its mysterious numbers and symbols, had brought forth something that neither Ric nor I could have planned. This is how it happens. Gifts of genius reveal themselves as surprise, if we are willing to see them, then act, do our part, and bring them into manifestation.

I'm fascinated with the numbers seven and twelve, found over and over in Revelation. Charles Fillmore, the cofounder of Unity, taught that the number seven is the number of completion on the human plane. The number twelve represents completion on the spiritual plane. The intensive had lots of examples of sevens and twelves with symbols.

The book of Revelation, this book of sacred mystery, dances with colors, strange characters, and symbols. It is sometimes frightening for people, sometimes glorious. The four characters that Ric painted are found in somewhat different form in the book of Ezekiel in the vision of the heavenly chariot. It's also in Jewish rabbinical *merkabah* "chariot" literature. There is the strangeness of the "eyes all over, front and back" that suggests an unusual and all-knowing awareness.

Interestingly, I'm also feeling a vague remembering of this image with thousands of eyes, as if eyes are all over our being, in some ancient Eastern poetry or scripture. These moments of remembering just come sometimes, as if connecting past, present, and future as one.

At various times, I've studied what scholars and teachers have said about it. It is clear, however, this has not been the way that my unique self seems to choose to open into its mystery. That kind of study takes me into the left brain, and it scrambles in the rational mind. The revelation that comes alive, for me, always seems to come through my right brain filled with color, creativity, and knowing that comes from beyond the rational mind. Maybe Ric and I are more alike than he realizes …

It will come, for me, profoundly in the synergy of the experience of "When two or more are gathered …" in a field opening to revelation. Words simply come to be scribed and shared, if we are willing, revealing different pieces of vaster expression. Ric's willingness to share happened more privately, after the intensive completed, while others were preparing to leave. We feel our own hesitancies.

I'm remembering now the documentary film *Into Great Silence*. It came to American theaters in 2007. German filmmaker Philip Gröning actually wrote to the Carthusian order of Monks for permission to make a documentary about them in 1984. They said they would get back to him. Sixteen years later, they were ready.

My response to *Into Great Silence* when I saw it shortly after it opened was simply awe. There were not a lot of people in the theater, and yet the space was full with the great silence. I've never forgotten it, even when the movie seemed to disappear.

The soundtrack for the movie has now been released in its entirety. It is a collection of chants, readings, prayers, and sounds of silence recorded by Philip Gröning during his six-month stay at the monastery. He says, "This Office of the Night appeared to me to be the core of the Monks life and spirituality, the heartbeat of the Order for more than a thousand years. I wanted to share my experience with an audience."

I told Ric it could really be deep, and also fun, if he would like to work with me on the four symbols from Revelations, the characters in his painting. We could do it like dream work. He was interested, said he'd like to do that. We'll see if it happens. These kinds of things are not to be pushed.

## Practice: Bringing Your Life into the Curriculum

Have you ever had responses to Revelations? Do you have hidden talents, gifts of genius, which come from imprints of the soul, that you don't really talk about or let people see? Are there hidden yearnings that you may not quite understand?

Have you ever been told by some authority figure, like a parent or a teacher, that this was not something that you could ever make money with, not a way to support yourself? Have you felt, or did someone tell you, that it wasn't good enough? Has this attraction or yearning continued to be there anyway?

How are you able to hear or experience the impulses, the whispers of your soul? What practices have you explored, seriously or casually?

How have symbols been a part of your life? Do you have sacred symbols? Do certain numbers or colors hold profound and significant meaning for you, attracting you in ways that guide you in bringing things into manifestation?

What is your natural way to record what comes? Will you choose something that compels you and draw, paint, write, scribe, or bring it into the manifest in your unique self way? Are you willing to share it? Or will it remain in the great silence?

Has your relationship with these ethereal mysteries changed in the different stages of your life? Have you ever pondered these things in your heart? Are you ready?

# CHAPTER 37

## *The Trimesters of Our Lives*

THERE ARE SO many meanings and moments in time when I think about the trimesters of my life. They span the spectrum from unknown meaning to childbirth and to meanings that take me into the vastness beyond.

Again it seems important to review. It helps us realize the immense gifts of our lives and imprint on our hearts even greater awareness of potential and destiny, ways we are still called to greater purpose.

And as I review the gifts that clearly are immensely significant for me, let it be with the awareness of invitation. I will invite you to give yourself that same gift of reviewing and identifying for yourself those immensely significant pieces of your life tapestry. It will lead you to even greater awareness of your potential, destiny, and ways that you are called to greater purpose.

The creation story of my childhood became the Codes of Co-Creation in this otherworldly process spanning many years. Out of that came the focus now of there being three trimesters. I am experiencing the feeling of being drawn to diving into higher and deeper realms, especially the vastness of the beyond.

The word "involution" was introduced into this sacred mystery, for me, when in the first six weeks of seminary, we opened into the creation story found in the Bible. Few people realize there are two different creation stories. Involution is what I call the descent of Spirit or sometimes the descent of the dove.

Adam and Eve in the Garden of Eden come in the second chapter of Genesis. It is very different. It includes what for some is called "the fall." It's what I call separation from our knowing of Oneness. We forget who we are. From this second chapter in Genesis clear through to the end of the Bible, the story of evolution as consciousness unfolds. Our learning how to live it takes a lot longer than the imprinting!

The words of one of my teachers, Marvin Anderson, imprinted me with Awareness and Being.. "This is the key to everything, and we don't understand it yet" opened my mind into a heart that seemed to already know and say yes to the mystery that will continue to reveal itself for the rest of my life and beyond.

That emergence led into three decades of teaching the Codes of Co-Creation, which clearly revealed themselves as occurring in three different realms of time, even while occurring simultaneously, always already, in the eternal realm of timelessness.

The three trimesters include the awareness of a mystical trinity: Spirit, soul, and body, embodied as you or me in this lifetime. The oneness of Spirit, invisible, cosmic, and transcendent, is always already present, even when I don't realize it, simply because it is beyond my human understanding.

My individualized soul is eternal, and it is the field through which so many of the glimpses of purpose and destiny come. It offers to bring the imprints of the soul into my physical body and being. It knows the lessons and soul assignments that I have come to learn and teach in this lifetime.

Our individualized souls are different from each other's, even while the Spirit within us is one. Our greatest perceived differences show up in the physical. We have so many different disguises, some quite delightful, some we could call strange and interesting! It occurs to me that it is a bit like Halloween, the day I happen to be writing this! Halloween is actually our rendition of All-Hallowed Eve coming before All Saints and All Souls Days. It's fascinating how we reinvent things!

In the first creation story of Genesis 1, we are taken into the mysteries of the invisible. It is stunning to become aware that it begins with "darkness" and is "without form and void." How many times have we experienced darkness, formlessness, and the void in our lives?

Each day in the sequence of seven days begins with "evening." The darkness is called night. In the night experiences, for me, things may not seem clear, may even feel unsettling or confusing. I sometimes can't see my way.

The light is called day. In the light, I have found my bearings, feel more confident and can go into action. After the first day sequence is described, we find the phrase, "So the evening and the morning were the first day."

The words, "So the evening and the morning ..." are repeated again for each of the six "days." We transcend what we have known, engage and emerge into another realm of vastness that we have not previously understood perhaps, except maybe in glimpses. And, we include the good, true and beautiful of our lives.

The phrase that emerged for me for these sequences is Codes of Co-Creation. I used to simply call it Codes of Creation. However, I began to profoundly realize, nearly twenty years ago, that it requires a coming together in co-creation. It is Spirit partnering with me in the process! Otherwise, my unconscious mind can easily block the process, the fulfillment of soul potential, and even destiny.

Can you tell that I've taken at least a thousand deep dives into this ancient navigational map of the cosmos? Can you see that the word thousand is deeply interwoven into my mind and heart as a symbol of the Power of One going into infinity? When thousand is written as the number 1,000 the one represents, for me, the Power of One and the zeros represent that power going into infinity.

I interrelate it now with science and the billions of years of evolution in time that, for me, dissolve into timelessness. The way of transcend and include has dissolved contradictions of faces, places, and experiences that I could not understand with my human mind.

Integral and the spiral, including the double spiral going higher and deeper, are part of my vastness. Every time I emerge into another higher level of light, that light shines its light on anything left unfinished in a corresponding level of the deeper darkness. It involves healing, often mind-blowing experiences, and integration.

The waters of Genesis 1:2 are, for me, the unconscious. I find it very comforting and calming to know that Spirit is *hovering over the face of the waters!* It means there are no accidents in the ways that things happen in my life. Even in my experience of the unbelievable or unbearable, there is a higher plan. My awareness of Romans 8:28 also anchors me in this knowing that all things work together for good for those who love.

You may still be wondering about all this scripture stuff, feeling like it is not you or at least a bit strange to you. It is part of the imprint of my soul. And if you have gone with me into our lives as a sacred love story, maybe you have also found it of value, or even amazing! Maybe later you will, and maybe you won't. You don't need to; there are many paths. Sometimes this whole process requires a bit of dialogue, mostly with yourself.

I have a scripture, interestingly, that I often go back to when things happen that seem impossible to deal with. It requires believing even when I can't, of my human self, do that with the unbearable. It is a story about a man asking Jesus for his son to be healed. The first question is "Do you believe?" The response is so deep, "I believe, help my unbelief." The story is found in Mark 9:23–24.

I haven't always been able to just dive into the amazing. The death of my own son and of my beloved were both times where my left brain went offline. The knowing of the whiteboard of my life being erased was overwhelming. What happened for me was that my right brain, my creative mind, knew how when my rational mind could not.

What I feel now is that a sort of rewiring of the brain took place in that void of my life that seemed to dissolve everything. Out of it has come a new story, a creation story that is beyond anything that I could have humanly imagined.

It seems to have prepared the way, in part, for potential deep dives with you and others, if there is a willingness to say yes to the invitation to see your life as a sacred love story.

## Practice: Bringing Your Life into the Curriculum

If you have taken the deep dives, you will be gaining new levels of seeing and knowing that you've never experienced before. At least that is the way it has been for me and continues to be. Even this morning, I saw new things, new ways to say it, in the first chapter of Genesis!

Did you bring into your mind different times in your life of darkness, of void, and of light? You would not have had to write in detail; you may not even want to now. You may still not even want to go there. Honor that, if that is what comes.

Also notice things that you believe or don't believe. Just notice. Jot it down. Feel into where the *believe* or the *not believe* came from. Did it come from your own heart or from something or someone else? Just be aware. Awareness will ultimately replace your thinking! First comes awareness, and after that, ultimately Awareness of awareness.

We are in the last stage of our journey in the garden together, a time perhaps to ask, for you and maybe even for the planet, where are you, where are we?

What is our purpose? Did you map the stages or decades in these realms of mystery? Did you think about the human completions? Can you also see your continuing journey of spiritual completions or even completions of another kind? Maybe it will involve commitments to social or planetary change in this time of planetary crises. What are your unique gifts or genius? How would they apply?

As you have gone into the process, do you see how it leads you? I'm hoping that you continue to scribe and write, simply because I know that if you do, it could be a gift for future time. And I am hoping that you say yes to being part of the tipping point that will change the world.

I invite you to go into the stillness, and in the pause between the breaths, in and out, invite the movement of the All That Is. What is the one purpose that you would fulfill in this immensely important, and for me, holy plan?

Or we might ask it in the way that it asked me: "If you could do anything in the world, what would it be?"

Scribe what comes …

# CHAPTER 38

## *When You Come to the Edge*

I HAPPENED TO see a post on Facebook this morning: "When you come to the edge, the magic begins …" The sea, the towering cliff, the starkness of mystery and what felt like danger were all things I related to. It was very powerful. That happened even as I recognized the word magic and the light in the picture as also familiar.

Even now I feel a new Self arising. Sometimes it feels so wide and unknown that it is disorienting. It feels like there are fewer and fewer people that I can even talk with about it. So I write.

And some of you respond, as Kathy Hill from the East Coast did this morning. Then, even more awareness comes in feeling the connection! The edges and the magic somehow seem to go together. I've come to trust that, even when it is still in the invisible.

The magic, for me, happens over and over. It plays hide and seek often, in all of its textures and flavors. It is part of every color of the rainbow, dancing in all of its sensual and passionate ways. What are the colors of words for you?

There is deep purple in the richness of symbols and tradition that calls to my heart, resonates with my soul. I love the color blue, a symbol for me of knowing the way. Red, for me, is the color of creativity and passion, giving the gift of experiencing the play and preciousness of coloring outside of the lines! It gives me tastes of delight and depth, of the unique and authentic that feels real. It plays with opposites and finds its way to the synergy that is beyond.

More colors become like a breastplate, like the breastplate of the high priest in ancient scripture, as I experience them in the realms of the heart. The wedding ring that my father gave my mother had rubies on each side of a diamond. Sapphire, amethyst, and emerald are included in this heart-knowing of love that is beyond time. Yellow becomes the gold of the circle without beginning or end.

Listening with the heart brings the awareness of the precious moments, the treasures that are forever love. All that is unlike that love simply dissolves in its purity, its magic, and its mystery.

Moments in time have revealed their own eras, and the propensities and complexities that are part of the human plane, as well as part of a universe and a story of Spirit, soul, and body. It is a rich and beautiful tapestry.

I've followed the dots and the points of light that have so profoundly guided me. It didn't always turn out the way I thought it would, although in the unfolding, it always revealed what I would later understand as part of the journey of the soul.

Yet still, I find myself coming at times "to the edge" of my knowing. There are places where it just doesn't compute, and I can feel my mind scrambling and even going offline. Somehow it seems important to record some of these passages, which are coming from this Awareness of another kind. It feels like they might be guides for others who travel these kinds of passages, which can feel strange or even daunting.

I've seen double rainbows enough to know they exist, even though they are rare! And my heart knows there are twelve precious gems in the breastplate of love. Are there colors of the rainbow that my human eyes do not see? Is it a replicating process, like double rainbows repeating in tiers beyond?

There is magic and simplicity now, knowing I am loving all of it simultaneously, all of the colors of the rainbows in their repeating reiterations, yet each one with greater and more clear soul awareness.

So, sometimes I dance purple and tradition, rituals and symbols manifest as love available in all of the stages of my life. Other times I may play with the orange brilliance of a sunrise, highlighted with coral. Achievement and success are words I've associated with orange magic, yet with the awareness of sunsets to come.

There is a turquoise magic out of which co-creation and collaboration arise. It holds the honoring, tenderness, and delight of the "we," when two or more are gathered ... in this field, with the knowing of a work that is not work. There is a profound beauty of the beloved embracing the beloved here.

The indigo and the violet realms give me the immense gift of knowing the Cave of the Heart, the invisible, as well as past, present, and future as one. The comfort and stillness of its magic hold me in its vastness.

This week I reread an old e-mail from my beloved Liza Tilson, now in her nineties. We are having lunch on Monday. She told me, "I used to like it better when you told stories. I could always relate them to my life." I have tried to do that in writing about stages of manifestation. Sometimes it doesn't come easily.

Maybe it will now. It is easier seeing it as all the colors of the rainbow. And it will be delightful to see the edges that have taken me into the magic of new colors!

## Practice: Bringing Your Life into the Curriculum

If you were to see your life as all of the colors of the rainbow, how would you describe the different stages? You could play with decades or even seven-year cycles of time. I invite you to try it! It has the elements of poetry, art, and beauty.

Are you experiencing double rainbows where replicating patterns or qualities such as safety, and security, or even where finding a tribe feels important? Can you see it?

# CHAPTER 39

## *From Glory to Glory*

TIME PASSES IN our horizontal perception into timelessness. And the mirrors that we look into reveal ages and stages, our own and of others that are part of our lives and world. Sometimes messages or lessons seem to come back, repeat themselves. Each stage is a hologram, learning repeating at higher octaves.

My deep connection to phrases from scripture comes back to guide me. The phrase that simply drops in again is "From Glory to Glory." Still, I don't remember where the verse is. I've forgotten. Did I also forget the deeper meaning that it wanted to give me? So I turn to the jotted-down favorite verses on what once were blank pages, now full, at the back of my Bible.

"But we all, with unveiled face, beholding as in a mirror the glory of the Lord, are being transformed into the same image from glory to glory …"

I find the verse again in 2 Corinthians 3:18. So many times I have gone to these pages where I have written the text references for words that so profoundly held personal meaning for me. These words and phrases are beacons of light that seem to speak to me from beyond.

Once again, the words are connecting very deeply in my being. My heart makes a simple translation of the word Lord, and the glory of the beloved fills me. Beholding it as in a mirror, I am transformed into the same image, from glory to glory. I experience, as this happens, all of the stages, shifts, and changes of my own life. I am resting in the realization of the All That Is.

A soft smile and a knowing of the sea changes come. The horizontal experience of time, as past, present, and future shifts. What emerges is vertical awareness of multiple realities existing simultaneously. I see my life as all of the dazzling colors of the rainbow, with even the knowing of double rainbows.

I'm remembering a time, years ago, when someone told me that my life seemed to move from glory to glory. What I thought it meant then was very different from what I've come to experience that it means now.

The complexities of change and choice are viewed somewhat differently from other times in my life. It is like being on a higher platform. Now there is a vaster seeing and Awareness of awareness with duality and non-duality as part of it.

What I see is a double spiral of higher and deeper. As we transcend and include in our soul journey, we embody higher vibrations of light. That light shines on deeper levels, density and darkness, in order for it to heal and dissolve. I know this is the power of light and love, conscious and unconscious.

Out of this maturing in worldviews has come a very deep and profound knowing of the significance of our lives as a sacred love story. We begin to see love, choose love, and ultimately live love, experiencing our very lives as the living flame of love.

The words sound easy. After all, who would not want love? Yet, what has existed, for me, has been a path filled with higher and deeper complexity, light and dark, joy and sorrow … until it all dissolves back into the total simplicity and glory of love.

I've lived the interrelationship with that other phrase used by mystics who have found and sometimes scribed the maps of this journey. That equally sacred phrase, *to die before you die,* doesn't seem to be about glory always.

With Awareness of awareness in my own life as both a human and a spiritual journey, I see so clearly those points of birth, death, and rebirth that have occurred and reoccurred in the stages of my own unfolding. It feels almost like I've lived multiple lifetimes in one lifetime.

Magic and mystery, delight and grief have been there. Knowing at different moments in time has dissolved into unknowing. Attraction and manifestation have dissolved in time. What has not dissolved is the love, visible and invisible, that is forever.

I have lived tsunamis, earthquakes, and womb houses, even while simultaneously knowing forever love. The choices seem, for me, choice-less choices. And change is still emerging, now more than five years after my last big cosmic erasure, in this journey without distance.

There is a wondering of what the more that is to come will be. Yet, I feel a smile as response, with the awareness of the always-already repeating patterns of the good, true and beautiful. A soft laugh comes as an experience of Joy.

# Practice: Bringing Your Life into the Curriculum

Take some time to sit in the stillness with a pen in your hand. Ponder the questions. Go into your heart and ask. Listen to the whispers that may come.

Are there pieces or phrases of sacred scripture or texts that somehow have become your favorites and have come into your awareness to guide you? Might there be, if you looked for them? Have they come more than once, repeating over and over again?

Open into letting the phrase "from glory to glory" reveal itself to you, unveiled. Would it have meant different things at different stages in your life? Have you experienced sea changes? Do you look at past, present, and future in your life with horizontal or vertical awareness? Can you conceive of these being part of the now moment, all existing simultaneously?

Do you experience greater and greater levels of complexity as your life evolves? Has there been a point where it began to dissolve back into simplicity and even love? Rest in the realization.

Scribe what comes …

# CHAPTER 40

## Love in the Mystery:
## A Vaster Vision

THE MYSTERY OF love, for me, has been visible and invisible, complex and simple. It feels beyond understanding with my human mind. Simultaneously, I feel still an immense curiosity that invites, even pulls me to know its secrets.

There are some things that have become clear as I have taken the deep dives of understanding stages and consciousness in my own life. Transcend and include are alive and well. And the yearning to know the mystery continues.

It has taken me into realms of co-creation that I could never have imagined. It has required surrender into unknowing. It has come in ways I could not or would not plan. It often starts with curiosity, a kind of attraction and invites action.

Sometimes there are assignments. Such an assignment was given to me in one of my early coaching and mastermind settings.

I was learning how to create my first telesummit, which became www.LivingLovingLegacy.com. Brett Thomas and Ewan Townhead were my guides.

The assignment was simple. Watch the TED Talk video of Simon Sinek called "Start with Why" and then figure out your own why. I took the leap into going higher and deeper. Why did I feel so strongly about love? The answer would become the beginning of a mission statement that would guide and lead.

## A Vaster Vision: Love in Your Life and in the World

First we *believe*, then we *know*, and then we *act*.

I believe that love is the most powerful force in the universe for healing lives, building dreams, and realizing the essence of the All That Is. The power of love goes beyond anything that the world has ever known.

Love forms a conveyor belt in its various stages, states, and incarnations. It does not separate in its healthy forms, and it awakens us even in unhealthy forms. It has the potential of bringing meaning and abundance to all.

Faces of love are found in our relationships, lovers, partners, friends and family; our work, vocation, or avocation. Love is found in our passion for transformation, for nature or creation, or whatever is unique to you.

Love in all of its forms will play an essential role in generating revolutionary ideas and solutions that will lead to the revelation of essence Itself.

I believe that love is a tipping point for a historic shift and that, individually and collectively, we can be part of the shift that brings into our lives the good, the true, and the beautiful.

Love is a field, a doorway that exists to connect people to love in its fullest potential. It exists within each individual, and in the we space of relationships. It emerges into knowing the essence of the All That Is. It is heaven on earth in emergence.

Love is an energy field that exists in the visible and the invisible. It yearns for us, even as we yearn for it. It pulls us with its vibration and catapults us beyond our limited and partial perceptions into vaster dimensions. It opens our partial seeing to clear vision as our souls go higher and deeper in the spiraling circles of life.

Love's teachings will transcend and include, transforming thinking and feeling, healing and shifting perceptions. As human awareness and soul awareness integrate, co-create, and dance, the process is synergistic, supporting the elevation of humanity through love.

Interestingly, a friend of Brett Thomas, who is also a coach, was a participant in this online gathering. There was an otherworldly moment when Jim Vollett and I discovered that we both had been deeply imprinted by Marvin Anderson, my teacher in ministerial school, who said, "This is the key to everything and we don't understand it yet." Jim had known Marvin years later in Vancouver and it had deeply influenced his life. These unlikely experiences of another kind feel like a message from Spirit affirming "I Am the Alpha and the Omega" of Revelation 22:13. In the beginning has taken on the vastness.

This morning, I turned my Scientific American 2016 calendar to the month of November. There is a beautiful space view from the Hubble telescope with an explanation of the photo. It is titled "Everything is illuminated: Light Echoes" and describes the expanding halo of light seen around a distant star. It is caused by illumination of interstellar dust from the red supergiant star at the center, which gave off an intense pulse of light in 2002. Called a light echo, the expanding brightness shows swirls probably caused by turbulence as the cloud slowly expands.

Suddenly, I'm feeling my own light echoes that can cause swirling in my own life, often creating a feeling of not knowing. There is an element of unsettling turbulence, even when I can recognize my own shifts in expanding consciousness. It is giving new meaning to this movement into the vastness. And, I find it fascinating that I've never read these explanations on my calendar in any of the previous ten months. And, today I did.

The Codes of Co-Creation and unveiling our sacred love story have seemed, for me, like a strange and yet a magnificent obsession! There have been many facets in this amazing journey. I can see it as a combination of the sacred and the human. And then I know it is all sacred.

It feels sometimes like I've lived John 12:24-26 with "Most assuredly, I say to you, unless a grain of wheat falls into the ground and dies, it remains alone; but if it dies, it produces much grain." I hear and experience the words "Follow me ..." and I know the profound meaning of that.

Simultaneously, there are moments when it is very human. I loved the song "Where You Lead, I Will Follow", which compelled me to get tickets for "Beautiful – The Carole King Musical" at the Segerstrom Center for the Arts recently!

Other moments, it feels like "I Am Woman" the song by the Australian-American artist Helen Reddy that was on her debut album released in 1971. That album also included "I Don't Know How to Love Him" and I feel the dissolve into that every time I hear it.

I can see that the journey has included all *Your Soul's Invisible Codes*, and all of the stages that we have explored in *Unveiling Your Sacred Love Story*. Love is the heart's whisper; it is the inspiration and the motivation that takes us into action and commitment. It is what moves us into true collaboration and ultimately into the Oneness when we have glimpses.

Now, I find myself coming back to John 12:32 and words that are deeply imprinted in my heart and soul: "And I, if I am lifted up from the earth, will draw all peoples to Myself." It feels like another iteration of an assignment that I know includes all of me.

## Practice: Bringing Your Life into the Curriculum

The question is: *how is your heart leading you?*

I've asked this question to hundreds, even probably thousands of people over so many years. I've followed my heart's lead and always have found its guidance to be true. And it is not always what my mind tells me! How has it been for you?

For me, it always is a profound moment that includes past, present, and future as one. It comes from the soul. It is a timeless knowing of the All That Is. It gives me awareness of a cosmic vastness in that moment. I feel a heart experience of joy and a peace that passes understanding.

It is the opening and the inviting of the descent of the dove. It is a causal field. It is the union of heaven and earth.

Interestingly, the next pieces seem to require the synergy of exploring. Our journey together holds the potential of leading us both into the next realms of the unexplored. It is a knowing, for me, of what happens "where two or more are gathered ..." We will potentially even be laying new cosmic grooves.

If we open into the highest levels, it will go beyond the rational mind and into the energy of visionary vibration.

I invite you to share deeply. How is it for you? What is your "why"? Does it start with the personal? Does it move into stages to the vastness? Finally, once more, go into the stillness and scribe what comes.

# Afterword

WHAT WILL HAPPEN in the after as we go forward in our lives? It has been, for me, such a profound in-the-world and not-of-the-world journey. It has unfolded over more than one year in time in the writing and over eight decades in the living!

On June 1, 2015, I made the commitment to write a Manifesto of Love over the next year. Commitments are very significant for me. Andrew Harvey and I were in a deep conversation about the unfolding of it. I had just been with him for a week as he led a retreat on mystical union. It ended with the writing of vows of an inner marriage and living it in the world.

On June 1, 2016, this manuscript was submitted to the publisher. It is a mirror of that promise and of our walking through the garden together. So many times we walked through the garden, pausing at Site 6, the Mystical Union.

Andrew Harvey and Marj at Site 6: Mystical Union

I am so aware of the power of passion, of attention, of recognizing words and symbols that are part of our path and destiny. Over ten years ago, Andrew was at Unity of Tustin doing an intensive on the way of passion and signed my copy of his book, *The Way of Passion, a Celebration of Rumi.*

The entire book is highlighted, with underlining and stars in addition! On page 157, Andrew is writing about commitments in our lives and passionately suggesting what that could mean. One sentence totally lit up for me:

"Set up educational institutions in which the sacred role of genius can be really known and understood and in which mystical discipline becomes the foundation of all the other disciplines."

Brilliantly clear and ecstatic, I knew the words were speaking directly to me, to my heart and my mind, to my purpose and passion.

It has been a passage that I've gone back to so many times, have taught and shared with others.

We can't know how the universe will weave together its surprises. We can know our intentions and commitment, even vows, to live our lives as a living vibration of forever love.

The garden amidst the flames has been a frame for so many stories, written and unwritten. You and I will live and potentially write more. The stories are parables of the magnificence, tenderness, courage, beauty, and wonder, fragments of a love story that are part of our very own unique thousand-piece puzzles.

My hope is that in our experience together, you have received some of what one of my teachers called "the key to everything." If you have, you will know that your life is a parable, a sacred love story that has codes that can be unveiled. You have had the eyes to see some of them; there are more to come.

My heart knows the meaning of the words of Mary Oliver: "When it's over, I want to say all my life I was a bride married to amazement. I was the bridegroom, taking the world into my arms."

I see dissolve, birthing and emergence, all qualities of Love. Each breath, glimpse, dream and vision holds the Love. Each is part of the opening, the guidance longing to be realized. It can be easy to miss, or to dismiss, in the environments where it is unseen, not recognized or misperceived.

One of the hardest, for me, has been letting go of forms that I have loved, so that new forms may appear. Some dreams have died and I have experienced the grief of loss. I haven't yet been able to see clearly the new visions that are there in potential. It is a time of unknowing. The glimpses of revelation and the prioritizing are still seeds to be nurtured. Often they take the form of yearning.

The way I thought it would turn out has somehow shifted in realms of universal awareness. Relationships, work in the world, even experiences of deep meaning are all subject to shifts beyond my human understanding.

Yet always there is the unfolding of our heart and soul, at times even more accelerated when our heart is broken open. New birthing knows its time and way, both visible and invisible.

When we started this journey together in Chapter 5, I wrote, "You will find more mystery. Within each stage of each of the seven years is the code of the seven stages. The microcosm is in the macrocosm in each of the stages. But that's too complex for now!" If you have taken the deep dives with these codes, you have seen some of the complexities of the mystery. Now we are at the Afterword.

What I have found is an Afterword and a sort of in-between time for all of the stages of my life. They are of the same Love Essence, including the dissolve into unknowing, the birthing and the emerging. Yet the forms are not the same, coming at times as surprise in the ways of the ordinary and extraordinary.

I am still feeling these amazing cycles replicating themselves, yet with higher and deeper ways of knowing. Now in my life, I am seeing the good, the true, and the beautiful in all of it. It has come to express in simplicity with an infinite grace. There is love, joy and a peace that passes understanding.

There is still more of the mystery, still invisible. It feels as if we may be co-creating some of what that is, together.

It is forever love.

## Practice: Bringing Your Life into the Curriculum

What is your Afterword now that is carrying you forward in your life? Are you flowing with it, like a river? Are you sometimes pushing the river?

Can you see stages that include dissolve, birthing and emerging, seeing with the eyes of love? Are your frequencies higher and deeper?

Do you feel the yearning that can carry the seeds of revelation, birthing and prioritizing to come? What is your Mystery of forever love?

I invite you to breathe into the Silence, align with your heart and simply scribe what comes.

# The Curriculum:
# Called By Love Institute
# and LOVE STAGES Inventory

## The Mission for Called By Love Institute:

"To harness the Power of love
    as a Revolutionary and Evolutionary Force,
Healing Lives, Building Dreams, Realizing purpose,
        destiny, and Legacy;
Connecting ordinary and extraordinary people
    to their fullest potential,
Bringing awareness and light into the world."

## What Does It Mean to Be Called By Love?

The curriculum for the work of Called By Love Institute is about consciousness and love as it *exists naturally*, in the form of *involution and evolution*, found in the developmental stages of our lives.

Love is one of the most powerful energies in the universe. It is in all of our lives in its developmental stages. There are pure forms as well as limited or distorted forms that appear differently as we grow and emerge in awareness in our human journey. It includes the good, the true, and the beautiful; it includes experiences of loss, jealousy, wounding, and grief. Poetry and love songs have been written about it since the dawning of time.

There are many faces of love. They show up as people, sometimes as avocation or vocation. If you ask someone, "What do you love?" there will be a multiplicity of answers, some personal and inner, some reflecting the outer and involving others. It is all part of the mystery of love.

The power of love has been felt by everyone. Yet the word has also been described to me as something that is fuzzy, even syrupy, with the suggestion that it is spoken of too lightly. There are just too many uses for it, some as casual as saying "I love ice cream."

Interestingly, even though there has been significant research on developmental stages over the last forty-plus years that has made a huge difference in understanding how consciousness works, to my awareness there has been nothing that focused on the interrelationship of developmental stages relative to consciousness and love. It seems to be in an unspoken void, too nebulous or too numinous to be taken seriously as a research subject.

Somehow the universe seems to have shaped it in different ways for me. My focus on curriculum at the University of Massachusetts happened because Dr. Robert Sinclair, chair of the Department of Curriculum, School of Education, found my work at the Feminist Press in New York and my background in public education a combination that was exciting and worthy of support. I am so grateful for his awareness and consciousness. It was an extremely important intersection in time.

I did not know that U Mass School of Education was doing some of the pioneering research in developmental stages. The work of Lawrence Kohlberg was part of my early exposure to something I had never considered. All of the rest would naturally follow, including the developmental stages in spiral dynamics, integral, the work of Dr. David Hawkins with his map of consciousness, as well as the double spiral of centering prayer, and work of Thomas Keating. It included the meeting of East and West. All of this would flow into my work with the stages of co-creation.

Now, Called By Love Institute offers transformative learning and teaching that *transcends and includes*, transforming thinking and feeling, healing and shifting perceptions, in the lives of ordinary and extraordinary people. Its work is about awareness, knowing human awareness and soul awareness integrate, co-create, and dance. The process is synergistic, supporting the elevation of humanity through love. It is about living, modeling, training, inviting, and initiating in the experience of a worldwide Campus of Consciousness committed to living your destiny, loving your life, and realizing legacy through love.

Called By Love focused first on monthly live intensives that took place on the campus of Unity of Tustin beginning in 2011. They gave me the freedom and the setting where I had the time to develop experiential curriculum and heal from the grief of tsunamis, earthquakes, and womb houses that I was experiencing in my own life. All of the intensives were recorded, both audio and video. I know these archives are still there for future time.

Then clearly part of the call became the co-creation of our first telesummit, with high-profile visionaries and teachers of consciousness, all of whom had been part of the Campus of Consciousness intensives developed over the nineteen years of my tenure as senior minister and CEO at Unity of Tustin. There had been 190 or more visiting master teachers during those years, and many became my dear friends.

When I received clear guidance to do a telesummit, something my human self did not know how to do, the guidance also gave me awareness of who to invite to be part of it. Included were Adyashanti, Andrew Harvey, Jean Houston, Russ Hudson, Roger Walsh, Constance Kellough, Don Beck, John Welshons, and James Twyman.

This esteemed group of spiritual teachers entered the co-creative field with me in our first telesummit. Constance Kellough, founder of Namaste Publishing, wrote: "Do not miss the most powerful parables of our time—the new scripture—shared by some of the world's leading spiritual teachers." Adyashanti invited me to come onto his worldwide broadcast just before our telesummit launch. The dialogue with Adya was about the descent of the dove. The list of people who became part of Called By Love's worldwide Campus of Consciousness emerged out of this field reflecting the amazing consciousness of incredible teachers.

Andrew Harvey, who had returned several times to Unity of Tustin for multi-day intensives, became the first speaker on www.LivingLovingLegacy.com. The dialogues, occurring in 2013, are all still available and part of the curriculum. This focus on elegant and scholarly work will continue to be included in the future.

The dialogues on Living, Loving, Legacy became part of the model for the curriculum that continues. Questions focused on the faces of love in each speaker's life and the power of this cosmic force beyond the human mind. The dialogues wanted models of the way of emergence, the spiraling path of destiny. Conversations of this kind in a series, to my awareness, had never been done before. Answers to the questions were deep and profound, about how it had all emerged in their own lives, including the difficult as well as the glorious! It wasn't about their work or gigs so much. It was about their lives.

Deep questions became the model for transformation that would emerge in this book, as well as in the Practices of Bringing Your Life into the Curriculum. I began to call it Write Your Soul, a phrase that I used when I wrote during my own time of immense grief, profoundly experiencing life-renewing guidance through the veils, from beyond my human mind.

Emergence continued with courses, from four to twelve weeks long. The month-long courses came first and included "Finding Your Golden Thread" with the awareness that it is coded into your life and that the codes can be unlocked, part of your own parable and sacred love story. Some examples follow; more will come.

"Love in the Spiral" invites the exploration of the map in our own lives, with the suggestion that it is like Lewis and Clark exploring the Louisiana Territory. We also recognize the natural times of pause in the flow of our lives, with choice points and glimpses of future destinations. "Where Are You? Where Are We?" explores the pause, knowing that it will lead us forth once again with renewed energy into the unknown, future synergy, and manifestation.

"How Is Love Looking for Work?" recognizes our yearning to do work that we love, often based on dreams and glimpses, even visions of what could be. We explore how love, the universe, the All That Is actually invites us, even yearns for us to embody it and manifest it. This deep dive into what it means to really build your own dreams and do the work you love is a dive into one of the faces of love that is other than romantic love!

"Kaleidoscope: Painting the Colors of the Rainbow in Our Lives" invites us to look at the thousands of revelations of light, the pieces of individual gifts of color that shift and change with the turning. They become the beauty and exquisite wonder of creation.

"Joy in the Unknowing" invited participants into a divine experiment of recognizing joy as one of the highest vibrations of consciousness. There are explorations in finding the questions, embracing paradoxes, being in the mystery, and following points of light. It is about connecting the visible and invisible, knowing the good, the true, and the beautiful, even as we have radical trust in the process. It is an invitation to the cosmic dance and cosmic play, loving the rainbows and the spirals. And it is knowing that the only way to lose is not to play!

Monthly worldwide calls with www.CalledByLoveInstitute.com are part of the curriculum. Themes are described in the e-mails that announce them. It is always about stepping into the living energy of emergence, the field that is alive with Source. It is about creation coming out of nothingness, no-thing-ness, the void, the dazzling darkness of non-dual awareness, or whatever you may want to call it.

Creation will emerge out of deep and profound conversations, inner and outer. There will be things that our human mind couldn't imagine, didn't intend, as well as support and energy for the things it did. Amazing depth of creative energy simply is brought into form. This is what happens when the energy of the unknowing is given its chance to express consciously.

## How Can You Be Part of the Co-Creation?

You will be part of the co-creation that is continuing to come into form now. One of the ways to enter into the field that is part of Called By Love is simply to register for the free calls that are community gatherings. All it requires is going to the website, www.CalledByLoveInstitute.com, and signing up to receive our e-mails. You may find also that you enjoy the regular blogs, with both voice recording and written transcript.

## Collaboration in a Greater Whole

The vision includes Called By Love Institute having faculty, many of whom will bring complementary pieces of a vision, with all of the parts being interrelated and collaborative in a greater whole. A synergy will exist in a co-creative field of emergence. This is the interconnection between the individual and the collective, with the power of love accelerating a global shift.

One of the examples of that emerging now is the development of the LOVE STAGES Inventory, which is in collaboration with Terri O'Fallon, a cofounder of Pacific Integral. Kim Barta is her co-teacher, a practicing therapist, and her brother. I kept hearing Terri's name, people telling me that she was someone that I needed to connect with, get to know, that she spoke my language. When those things happen in your life, listen. It can be an invitation from beyond!

The LOVE STAGES Inventory, available on www.Called ByLoveInstitute.com, is doing the groundbreaking research on the stages of love in human development. The research will stand on the shoulders of the significant work of Terri O'Fallon in her groundbreaking STAGES model, which helps you identify the level from which you habitually make sense of your experience and the world. Terri O'Fallon's work stands on the shoulders of those researchers who came before her, including Susanne Cook-Grueter and Ken Wilber. I feel such reverence and gratitude for all of the work that has come before with deep and rigorous research platforms.

This collaboration with master teachers in the birthing of the LOVE STAGES Inventory is an example of the kind of curriculum collaboration that I have been describing. It includes all of the elements: vision, dreams, radical faith and trust, glimpses of how it can happen. It invites willingness and action, even choices and surprises. Most of all, it invites love and wisdom and a monumental shift into realization and return. It requires that you bring your life into the curriculum, and it shows you a way, even invites you to provide your own data about where you are on the journey! It lives in a field of non-judgment and support, inviting you to play.

I believe that all of the stages of our lives are exquisitely part of what I call the colors of the rainbow. They are all there, consciously and unconsciously, visible and invisible, yearning for you to know the beauty of your being and the codes of your soul. They are part of the reason that you came to earth, to love, serve, and remember.

There are different languages for different countries, different ways of describing, different worldviews. You are invited to be part of describing the languages, how they love, how they serve, and how they remember. It is an invitation to stand on holy ground.

Marj Britt
June 1, 2016

# Acknowledgments

To ALL OF those beautiful souls who are part of Called By Love, past, present, and in future time: You are part of co-creating a template for humanity that will bring light and love into the world, healing and transforming it.

To the incredible core team of Called By Love Institute: You are visionaries, saying yes to that which is greater than ourselves and giving your gifts of genius, your time, talent, and treasures. You are co-creative midwives to the birth of a vision.

To the beloved Unity of Tustin community and team, past, present, and to come, and to Rev. Carolyne Mathlin who is leading Unity of Tustin now: You are giving gifts to future generations. I am so grateful for all of you and your continuing to carry this great light into the world.

To beloved Fabienne Meuleman, my Belgian daughter, co-creator and cherished playmate in this cosmic exploration: You are a miracle, given by the universe, simply a beacon of light and love. Your coming into my life was certainly a divine gift, something you and I could have never forecast or arranged, and you have been a breath of life in your pure essence of the All That Is.

To beloved Melanie Davis, angel of everything, including technology: You said, "You need a master mind partner," and then became one and so much more. You are a way shower, so deeply connected to the Holy Spirit. Together we bridge the worlds. Our virtual connection is a witness to the ways of the invisible.

To beloved Dr. Michael Ward, beautiful soul friend and confidant: How I have cherished our deep conversations over so many years and our explorations of worlds beyond. With you, India, Egypt, France, and Italy became lived experiences. In so many ways, we have been guides and support for each other. I know your incredible heart and soul.

To Vanessa Van Nieuwenhuysen and Karina Rindt, beloved angels of our invisible worldwide presence on Facebook, and to Kay Hultgren, our beloved angel of the visible: Your deep devotion and commitment to our posts and our live presence come from your hearts and the beauty of your souls. This web of light is part of "You are the light of the world." Our hearts are one.

To all of the beloved souls who are part of this sacred love story, you are cherished and acknowledged, even if not specifically named. You know who you are. You have been there in this sacred journey; we have been cogs in our connecting wheels of each other's lives. We know it and have lived it together. Because our intersections in time happened, there are gifts and blessings that have come into our lives. It truly is a wonderful world. I am in deep love and gratitude.

# Recommended Authors and Resources

I HAVE CHOSEN these resources because they are the ones that deeply inspired my own Awareness over three decades. They are ones that I recognize as profoundly shaping the journey that gave birth to 'Your Soul's Invisible Codes, Unveiling Your Sacred Love Story'. One of my great loves is books.

Over these decades, I have read, taught and used hundreds of books, most of which are still on my bookshelves. Yet the ones that are on automatic for me, and most directly related to this book, were relatively easy to choose. There are special reasons for each choice, stories about why. You will find and choose your own. These were some of my most profound guides at different points in the journey.

If you are interested in the stories, I've written about some of them after each of the author's bio material on www.LivingLovingLegacy. com. It is about 'Intersections in Time' that, if you notice them, can change your life.

Andrew Harvey. *The Way of Passion* (Frog, Ltd., 1994)
   *The Hope* (Hay House, Inc., 2009)

Don Beck. *Spiral Dynamics* (Blackwell Publishing, 1996) with Christopher Cowan
   *Spiral Dynamics Integral* (Sounds True, 2006) audio CD series

Ken Wilber. *Spectrum of Consciousness* (Theosophical Publishing House, 1977)
   *Grace and Grit* (Shambhala Publications, 1991)
   *Sex, Ecology, Spirituality: The Spirit of Evolution* (Shambhala, 1995)
   *One Taste* (Shambhala, 1999)

Roger Walsh. *Essential Spirituality* (John Wiley & Sons, Inc., 1999)
   *The World of Shamanism* (Llewellyn Publications, 2007)
   *Articles on A Course in Miracles* (drrogerwalsh.com)

*A Course in Miracles* (Foundation for Inner Peace, 1975)

David Hawkins. *Power Vs. Force* (Veritas Publishing, 1995)
   *Transcending the Levels of Consciousness* (Veritas Publishing, 2006)
   *Letting Go: The Pathway of Surrender* (Veritas Publishing, 2012)

Adyashanti. *The End of Your World* (Sounds True, Inc., 2008)
   *True Meditation* (Sounds True, Inc., 2006)
   *Resurrecting Jesus* (Sounds True, Inc. 2014)

Russ Hudson. *Personality Types* (Houghton Mifflin, 1996) with Don Riso
   *The Wisdom of the Enneagram* (Bantam Books, 1999) with Don Riso

Llewellyn Vaughan-Lee. *Love Is a Fire* (The Golden Sufi Center, 2000)
   *Fragments of a Love Story* (The Golden Sufi Center, 2011)

Sri Nisargadatta Maharaj. *I Am That* (The Acorn Press, 1975)

Satprem. *Sri Aurobindo or The Adventure of Consciousness* (Institut de Recherches Evolutives, Canada, 1996)

Jack Schwarz. *Human Energy Systems* (E. P. Dutton, 1980)

John Steinbeck. *Sweet Thursday* (Viking, 1954)

Eric Butterworth. *The Creative Life* (Tarcher/Putnam, 2001)

Myrtle Fillmore. *Letters of Myrtle Fillmore* (Unity School of Christianity, 1936)

Charles Fillmore. *Prosperity* (Unity Books, 1936, 1983, 19th printing) *The Twelve Powers*, 1st edition (Unity Books, 1930) combined with Cora Fillmore. *Christ Enthroned in Man* (Unity Books Classics, 1999)

Ernest Wilson. *The Week That Changed the World* (Unity Books Classics, 2006)

Evelyn Underhill. *Mysticism* (Meridian, 1974)

*Bible.* King James Version is my favorite, and is used for quotes in this book.

Marj Britt. *Stillness* This is my Greatest Resource. Sitting in the Silence is when Downloads come most readily. Scribing comes out of this. I call it being aware of the breath, listening to the whispers or 'Write Your Soul'.

# About the Author

DR. MARJ BRITT is a mystic in the world, a master teacher, with consciousness and love as the living flame of her life. She is the founder of Called By Love Institute, a worldwide Campus of Consciousness, at www.CalledByLoveInstitute.com.

Marj was the visionary leader of Unity of Tustin, California, for nineteen years. Widely known for its beautiful meditation gardens and as a Campus of Consciousness, Unity of Tustin hosted during her tenure as senior minister some of the foremost master teachers of today.

In September 2011, Marj founded Called By Love, out of which a telesummit, www.LivingLovingLegacy.com was birthed, even while also continuing to offer live intensives monthly at Unity of Tustin. It is about how to recognize the faces of love in your life, past, present, and future, all in the now, as one.

Called By Love is centered in the mystery of the template of love as creation, in all of the stages and states of your life. It invites you to identify your soul spiral and the center of gravity shifts in your life and to know what is always already. Your personal map of creation is the revelation of your own cosmic and human love story. It is your spiritual autobiography of love in all of its wonderful and strange forms.

Marj holds a doctoral degree from the University of Massachusetts School of Education with a focus in curriculum, psychological education, and counseling. Her dissertation was on "Life Patterns of High Success Women." The School of Business was represented on her dissertation committee as an outside member. She attended seminary at Unity School of Christianity and was ordained in 1988. Marj has served on the Unity Institute seminary board, the Academic Governance Council, as well as in other national leadership roles.

# Introduction to
# the 1,000 Entries Index

ONE INTENTION OF an index, and the usual one, is to assist in locating persons, places and important concepts or teachings. It leads you to where you can find things in a book. As I have worked with identifying these items for the index, I've experienced many deep feelings of gratitude for all that has been and for all that will come.

This index, however, is intended to serve purposes beyond the usual. I have been a passionate teacher of experiential learning for many years. The stories, memoir, or parables in the book and the questions at the end of each chapter are all about that. It is about bringing your life into the curriculum.

As I have identified themes and concepts for the index, I realized nearly all of them could become experiential practices. There are 1,000 entries. You know my passion for the one thousand-piece puzzle. It feels to me that this index is kind of a magical toolbox! My invitation to you is to look through the index and see how the energy of different entries draws you. Some may even light up and intrigue you with curiosity.

Designing your own experiences around these will be a creative process, perhaps an initiation coming from your soul. Explore ways to apply the concepts to how your own life is happening. The index is for you to use and look for clues of the mystery in multiple ways. I invite you to consider some deep dive explorations!

# Index

## Symbols

180-degree shift in perception  59

## A

abandonment  30
accelerated learning process  146, 148
addiction  184
advanced students in our human
    bodies  82
Adyashanti  v, 75, 328, 336
A. H. Almaas  21
Allah  279
All I Ask of You  266, 267
All of the ways are right ways  285
All the Way  43, 44, 174, 247, 266
all things work together for good
    259, 294
Always Already  5, 16, 21, 39, 41, 47,
    50, 70, 77, 108, 110, 116, 153,
    157, 181, 205, 215, 292, 340
Amherst, Massachusetts  176

Andrew Harvey  xxi, xxiv, 22, 319,
    320, 328, 336
Andy and Cathy Blanton  101
Angels in disguise  112
angst  225
Are we there yet?  151
As above, so below  81
Ascent of the Soul  16, 118
Asilomar  75
as in a mirror the glory  305
Ask and you will receive  155, 257,
    265, 266
attention  x, xxiii, xxx, 92, 97, 101,
    103, 108, 118, 141, 146, 148,
    152, 204, 265, 270, 279, 320
attracting power of love  254
Aunt Lydia  10, 83, 203
authenticity  255
auto-responder  30
awakened in the night  226
Awareness beyond judgment  40
Awareness of awareness  xxiv, xxvii,
    187, 205, 255, 296, 306, 307

343

capitalization  xxvi, xxvii
Carl Jung  81, 179, 180
Carolyne Mathlin  333
Carolyn Mary Kleefeld and David
    Wayne Dunn  76
Carthusian order of Monks  287
Cast your bread upon the waters
    186, 190
catapults us beyond  313
Causal field  315
Cave of the heart  232, 279, 281, 301
center of gravity  45, 93, 97, 183, 339
cerebral palsy  78
Chan and Dyane de Cramer  280
Change happens  146
changing the world  162
chaos  209
chapel talk  165, 166, 167
Charles Fillmore  xxix, xxx, 58, 65,
    91, 119, 168, 179, 249, 286, 337
Chartres Cathedral  270
Children of Israel forty years to enter
    the Promised Land  xxviii
Choice-less choice  241, 307
choice points  329
choices shift and change  205
Choose once again  93, 141
choose our parents  173
Choose you this day whom you will
    serve  203, 204
Christian mysticism  226
circle without beginning or end  300
clarity  231
co-creation and collaboration  301
codes can be unlocked  329
Codes of Co-Creation  vi, xxix, 4, 5,
    22, 29, 111, 135, 153, 160, 262,
    291, 292, 294, 314
coincidences or signs  181
coloring outside of the lines  300

Colors of the rainbow  xxii, xxvi,
    xxvii, xxix, 23, 94, 110, 117,
    171, 177, 179, 180, 205, 214,
    215, 269, 301, 302, 306,
    329, 332
Come, Holy Spirit  39, 117, 220
comfort zones  204
Coming back into the marketplace
    with gift-bestowing hands  117,
    140, 160, 276, 280, 281
Coming of the Holy Spirit  102, 219
Commitment  xxii, xxiii, xxiv, 52,
    109, 111, 136, 151, 190, 195,
    196, 206, 209, 214, 216, 225,
    230, 262, 296, 315, 319, 320,
    321, 334
commitment to stay with the
    process  230
commitment to Transparency  225
compassion  viii, 249
compelled  75, 77, 314
complementary pieces of a vision  331
completed their purpose  141
completion  6, 135, 248, 286, 296
complexities  22, 36, 172, 196, 206,
    300, 306, 322
complexity dissolves into
    simplicity  110
confused self  79
confusion  47, 51, 78, 209, 221
connecting the visible and
    Invisible  330
Conscious Covenant  280
Constance Kellough  72, 328
contract with my soul  109
conveyor belt  xxiv, 95, 162, 168,
    172, 312
Cosmic Awareness  211
Cosmic Imprint  30, 271, 279
Cosmic Missions  162
Cosmic Vastness  17, 315

invisible Platform  xxiii, 79, 145, 146, 147, 160, 267
invisibly contained in each stage  xxxii
invitation  xii, xiii, xxiv, xxix, xxxi, xxxiii, xxxiv, 4, 10, 41, 46, 93, 111, 116, 222, 241, 280, 291, 295, 330, 331, 332, 341
invitation to say yes  241
invitation to the cosmic dance and cosmic play  330
invitation to write your own manifesto of love  xxxi
invocation  117, 215, 216, 221
invoke the promises  30
Involution  xxix, 16, 215, 278, 292, 325
Islam  84, 279
it is written on my heart  253, 254
It pulls us with its vibration  313

## J

jade table  89, 101, 102, 118
James Dillet Freeman  116
James Twyman  328
Janet Manning  xxix
Jean Houston  135, 139, 328
Jeff Walker  168
Jesus  xxvi, xxviii, xxx, 40, 77, 84, 85, 93, 160, 184, 279, 281, 295, 336
Jim Vollett  313
job loss  78
Joel Fotinos  226
John Robinson  157
John Stoesser  240, 246
John Welshons  51, 328
journey of manifestation  xxxii, 173, 179
journey of the soul  300
journey without distance  xxxi, 4, 69, 179, 307

joy and sorrow  38, 77, 307
Joy in the Unknowing  330
Judaism  84, 279
jumping off point  184, 189

## K

Kahlil Gibran  94
Kaleidoscope  329
Kansas City  104, 139, 175, 176, 179, 184, 214
Karina Rindt  xxxii, 334
Kathy Hill  x, 299
Kay Hultgren  334
Ken Wilber  22, 49, 59, 82, 94, 95, 281, 331, 336
The key to everything  15, 16, 29, 36, 292, 313, 321
Kim Barta  167, 169, 331
kind of manifestation  240
kinds of partnerships  248, 250
Kissing Darkness  76
knower within  24
knowing of multiple realities  31
knowing of the visible and invisible  241
knowing that comes from beyond the rational mind  287
knowing two or more realities simultaneously  199
koi pond  193, 204
Kosmic Consciousness  95

## L

Laughter  108, 228, 231, 259
Lawrence Kohlberg  327
laying new cosmic grooves  315
leading and guiding  152
leaves of the tree  278
lessons and soul assignments  293
lessons we've come to learn  173
let confusion dissolve  78

multiple realities existing
simultaneously xxxii, 6, 31,
40, 69, 79, 107, 220, 222, 235,
255, 306
mystery of anticipation 209
mystery of love xxxi, 212, 311, 326
mystic x, xii, xxiii, xxix, 16, 17, 22,
60, 72, 82, 183, 307, 339
mystical knowing 29, 81, 159, 175
mystical marriage 6, 237, 240, 245,
246, 250, 253, 254
mystical marriage within 254
Mystical trinity: Spirit, soul, and
body 292
mystical union 232, 237, 240, 246,
249, 319, 320

**N**

Namaste Publishing 328
Naropa University 82
Native American paths 279
natural vi, xxiii, 35, 37, 38, 45, 46,
51, 58, 103, 108, 141, 142, 179,
180, 188, 199, 228, 231, 261,
288, 329
natural times of pause 329
needle of our attention 265
Networking 134
network of guides 179
Nevada's Route 50 270
new birth 227, 231
new covenant 253
new creation emerges 117
new energies to come in 195
new paradigm 141, 154
new perceptions 50
new perspectives 50
New Self arising 299
next tribe is the world 211
Nicolaas-John van Nieuwenhuysen
xi, 281

no accidents 294
No Boundary 49
no control 229, 258
no details 45
Non-attachment xxiv, 255
non-demanding 241
Non-Dual 60, 172, 187, 249,
254, 330
Non-harmfulness 255
non-laws 255
nonsexist curriculum 176
no obstacles 221
no stones to trip on 221
not be a scholarly book xxx
not ego stories xxxi
nothingness 21, 24, 198, 330
not know 186, 327, 328
not the end of the journey 117
not time yet 227
not understood or appreciated 249
no wrong answers xxxii
numbers xxviii, 5, 6, 32, 118, 186,
187, 261, 285, 286, 288, 294
numbers seven and twelve 5, 286

**O**

odyssey 5, 59
of a different kind xxiii, 185, 241
offered to the world 72
old church in Paris 270
old paradigm will dissolve 141
olive trees 279
omniscience 198
one function 221
one soul 174, 175, 230, 266
only the shadow knows 154
on track 135, 179, 198, 200, 230
open circle 280
openness to receive 70
open your heart 177
oracle 29

286, 287, 288, 312, 313, 321, 323, 329, 340
rewiring of the brain 295
Ric Kolibar 284
right brain 287, 295
right brain, my creative mind, knew how when my rational mind could not 295
Robert Hudson 139, 271
Robert Sinclair 326
Roger Walsh 281, 328, 336
role model xi, 136, 179
Romans 8:28 xxii, 259, 294
romantic love 249, 329
Rumi xxii, 166, 320
rushing mighty wind 102, 219
Russ Hudson 109, 328, 336

# S

sacred love story vii, xii, xxv, xxix, xxx, xxxiv, xxxv, 41, 72, 146, 148, 152, 158, 169, 173, 180, 188, 206, 211, 219, 269, 272, 295, 306, 314, 315, 321, 329, 334, 335
sacred template 214, 216
sacred wedding within 111
sadness 108, 209
safety, and security 174, 302
Saint Francis 204
sand tray 83, 263
saying yes 69, 176, 333
scaffolding 166
schedule planned 145, 148
scribe xxxiii, 12, 17, 79, 105, 117, 119, 120, 137, 142, 149, 155, 162, 169, 177, 181, 190, 197, 206, 214, 216, 222, 228, 230, 251, 266, 267, 272, 288, 296, 308, 316, 323
sea changes 6, 306, 308

second monumental shift 225
seedpod 92
seeds of our soul's path of destiny 82
see in a mirror, dimly 64
seeing beyond the duality 77
seeing in a mirror darkly 107
seeing the dissolve 169
seeing through the eyes of love xxxi, 177, 188, 281
see the good 220
see visions 103
see with new eyes 231
selfless service 120
Seminary board xxiii, 159, 340
senior minister xxi, 39, 139, 159, 327, 339
seven chakras 5, 45
seven generations into the future xxxi
seven generations into the past xxxi
seven is the number of completion on the human plane 286
seven-year cycles 5, 32, 40, 70, 262, 302
shadow crashes 167, 254
Shantivanum 226
shape-shifted 179
shared path of destiny 248
shifted into a vastness 227
shifted my awareness of value 220
shift from one reality to another reality 199
shift from personality to individuality 180
shift into the fourth stage 152
The Shift Network 265
shift to a higher realm 147
shines the light on a deeper level of darkness 60
shorthand xxvii
signs 103, 111, 151, 177, 181, 186, 246

silent meditation retreats  23, 75, 117,
    139, 160
silent tears  64
silent words  64
Simon Sinek  312
simplicity  xxxi, xxxii, 46, 97, 110,
    120, 196, 214, 216, 248, 301,
    307, 308, 322
simultaneously conscious of both
    parts  229
simultaneously knowing forever
    love  307
skill at translating  103
soft launch  145, 151
song of your soul  69, 142
sorrow  xxxiii, 3, 11, 38, 47, 51, 76, 77,
    140, 258, 307
soul ascending  206
soul assignments  78, 79, 293
soul's DNA  70
soul's knowing  70
soul's plan  6, 38, 46
Sounds True  95, 336
sow your seed  186
space between the breaths  183
Space-Time and Beyond  118
spans several stages  232
speaking in different languages  219
Spectrum of Consciousness  22, 49,
    205, 336
spiral  xxii, xxiii, xxx, 3, 23, 44, 45,
    59, 60, 66, 109, 135, 136, 146,
    147, 152, 177, 187, 228, 260,
    262, 294, 306, 327, 329, 330,
    336, 339
Spiral Dynamics  23, 59, 109, 136,
    177, 327, 336
spiraling higher and deeper  60, 146
Spirit  xxvi, 16, 30, 31, 39, 81, 102,
    103, 104, 105, 107, 108, 112,
    115, 117, 118, 120, 135, 139,

140, 162, 206, 215, 219, 220,
    221, 222, 226, 248, 251, 253,
    257, 259, 262, 280, 292, 293,
    294, 300, 313, 334, 336
Spirit descending  206
Spirit, soul, and body  112, 115, 259,
    292, 300
spirituality  35, 287, 336
spiritual mountaintop  133, 134, 140
spiritual parents or children  85
spiritual partnership  140, 248, 262
spiritual practice  11, 120
spontaneity  266
Sri Aurobindo  198, 337
Sri Nisargadata Maharaj  197
stages  vii, xi, xii, xxi, xxii, xxiii, xxvii,
    xxix, xxx, xxxii, xxxiii, 5, 6,
    22, 23, 32, 33, 38, 40, 44, 45,
    46, 47, 50, 60, 61, 78, 86, 92,
    95, 96, 102, 109, 115, 116, 134,
    135, 136, 137, 139, 151, 152,
    160, 166, 167, 168, 169, 172,
    176, 177, 179, 180, 183, 184,
    186, 187, 189, 198, 204, 205,
    211, 214, 215, 216, 231, 232,
    240, 254, 255, 281, 288, 296,
    301, 302, 305, 306, 307, 308,
    311, 312, 315, 316, 322, 323,
    325, 326, 327, 331, 332, 339
STAGES inventory  vii, 23, 109, 167,
    168, 180, 198, 211, 325, 331
Stages of Co-Creation  xxi, 33, 327
stages of the Double Rainbow
    replicate in higher ways  180
stained-glass  240, 241, 245
Star of David  279
star seed transmissions  70
States and stages  xi, 22, 40
stepfather  174
Stephanie Dowrick  226
stepping-stones  45, 66, 134

Thomas Hübl  69, 141
Thomas Keating  23, 60, 109, 327
thousand  xxiii, xxx, 21, 44, 58, 71,
    84, 93, 96, 125, 133, 169, 181,
    184, 186, 286, 287, 294, 315,
    321, 329, 341
thousand-piece puzzle  21, 44, 71, 96,
    125, 169, 181, 321
three paths of Abraham  84, 279
three phases or tiers  xxxii
Thy will  179
ticket punches  184
Till the End of Time  269, 271
time in the stillness  190, 222,
    231, 254
time in the womb is essential  227
Timelessness and time  102, 105, 196
time of cosmic shift and
    realignment  226
time of immense acceleration  133
tipping point  59, 296, 312
to die before you die  230, 307
to learn and perhaps to teach  81
to let go  79, 210
to lose entirely all interest in
    knowledge  198
Tom Zender  280
tongues  102, 103
tools  vi, 109, 111, 258
top choice  206
total simplicity  307
tradition  xi, xxx, 71, 77, 124, 221,
    262, 300, 301
tradition, rituals and symbols  301
transcend and include  51, 60, 84,
    95, 160, 196, 277, 294, 306,
    311, 313
transcending and including  81,
    84, 248
transcribe  125, 155

transformative learning and
    teaching  327
transforming thinking and feeling,
    healing and shifting
    perceptions  313, 327
translation  xxvii, 31, 188, 204, 205,
    259, 306
tree of life  278
triangle  108, 109, 111, 112, 115
Trinity  22, 37, 112, 115, 214, 216,
    259, 292
true north  108
Tsunamis, earthquakes, and womb
    houses  140, 225, 307, 327
Turn, Turn, Turn  184
turquoise magic  301
twelve fruits  278
twelve precious gems  301
twelve represents completion on the
    spiritual plane  286
twelve stages  186
twin souls  175
two monumental shifts in my life  220
two non-identifiable beings of
    light  239
two polarities can exist
    simultaneously  210

# U

UC Irvine medical students  281
U Mass  135,.139, 165, 176, 211, 327
unbelievable or unbearable  294
unconscious  50, 60, 78, 81, 91, 94,
    104, 147, 184, 205, 215, 216,
    294, 306
unfinished business  79, 172, 173
union of heaven and earth  6, 315
union of love and wisdom  247
union of the opposites  94
unique gifts  69, 72, 296

# Y

# Z

Printed and bound by PG in the USA

USA2019PGIL